This Too Shall Pass

A Memoir of Survival, Loss, and Finding Purpose

LORETTA A. OBERHEIM

For information about the author:
www.lorettaoberheimart.com

Copyright © 2025 Loretta Oberheim

All rights reserved. No part of this book may be reproduced or used in any form or manner whatsoever without written permission except in the case of brief quotations for articles and reviews.

ISBN: 9798312416619

Independently Published Design and Composition: Loretta A. Oberheim
Cover: "11:04", mixed media painting on canvas by Loretta A. Oberheim.

DEDICATION

This book is dedicated to those who have weathered life's storms— the resilient souls who have faced loss, fear, and adversity yet found the strength to keep moving forward. May these pages serve as a beacon of hope, a reminder that your journey, no matter how difficult, is meaningful.

To my beloved family and cherished friends, your unwavering support has been my anchor. Your love, encouragement, and belief in me, even when I doubted myself, have been my guiding light. I am forever grateful for your presence in my life.

To every survivor navigating their own struggles, know that you are not alone. Our pain, resilience, and hope connect us all. Healing is possible, and reaching out for support is an act of courage.

To my husband, Kenny—my rock, my safe haven—your love and unwavering faith in me have been my greatest strength. Thank you for always seeing the best in me.

To my parents, for their unconditional love and belief in me, and to my siblings, John, Sal, Justin, and Marie, for their laughter and companionship—thank you for being my foundation and my joy.

To my fur children – Delilah, Winston, Shea & Anna. Thank you for allowing me to fulfill my maternal side. But most of all, for the unconditional love when I didn't want to face reality.

And finally, to my own journey—the trials and triumphs, the pain and healing. Our scars are not marks of defeat but proof of our resilience. May this book stand as a testament to the human spirit's ability to overcome, to grow, and to find beauty in the brokenness.

CONTENTS

	Dedication	V
1	The Weight of Survival	Pg 1
2	Who I Was	Pg 5
3	The Crash – A Moment Between Worlds	Pg 9
4	The Nature of Grief	Pg 15
5	The Emotional Toll of Trauma	Pg 17
6	The Burden of Survivor's Guilt	Pg 25
7	Asking for Help – Strength in Vulnerability	Pg 35
8	Healing as a Choice	Pg 45
9	A New Diagnosis, A New Reality	Pg 49
10	Professional Patient – Navigating the U.S. Healthcare System	Pg 57
11	Rebuilding Identity	Pg 63
12	Finding Healthy Outlets – Redirecting Energy	Pg 69
13	The Spiritual Side of Healing	Pg 77
14	Relationships and Recovery	Pg 85
15	A New Beginning	Pg 93
16	Finding Joy in New Ways	Pg 99
17	Embracing Change – The Art of Letting Go	Pg 105
18	Art as a Symbol of Recovery	Pg 111
19	A Small Moment – A Big Win	Pg 115
	Epilogue – This Too Shall Pass	Pg 119
	Acknowledgements	Pg 125
	About the Author	Pg 129

CHAPTER 1:
THE WEIGHT OF SURVIVAL

Survivor's guilt is an insidious emotion, creeping into quiet spaces and settling into bones with an unshakable grip. It does not announce itself with clarity but lingers in the silence of sleepless nights, in the sudden pangs of guilt when laughter breaks through the sorrow, in the way the body tenses at the thought of moving forward. It whispers questions that have no answers: *Why me? Why did I survive?* It is a burden carried in the spaces between recovery and remembrance, between gratitude and grief. It is both a wound and a scar, something that heals and yet never fully disappears.

The moment my car was struck, my world fractured. Time slowed in an unnatural way, each second stretched and distorted. The weightlessness of the vehicle as it went airborne, the disorienting tilt of the world turning upside down and back again—these moments exist in my memory like frozen frames of a film. And then, stillness. The crushed metal cage around me, the distant sounds of sirens, the sharp scent of gasoline and blood. I was trapped, but I was alive. That fact alone became my torment.

After the accident, my survival felt unfair. I saw others whose lives had been permanently altered. People who had lost limbs, suffered brain injuries, or endured losses greater than mine. In comparison, my suffering seemed less, undeserving of the grief I felt. My pain didn't seem to be "enough." The doctors told me I was lucky. That I had walked away from something that should have ended me. But it didn't feel like luck; it felt like theft. As if I had stolen time I did not deserve, borrowed breaths that should have belonged to someone else.

But trauma is not a competition. Pain is not measured in degrees of suffering. Just because someone else's burden is heavier does not mean mine wasn't real or that I didn't have the right to grieve the life I lost. Because that's what it was—a loss. Not just of health and physical ease, but of security, of certainty, of the belief that life follows a predictable path. In its place was something fractured, a reality built on the fragile understanding that everything could be taken away in an instant.

The guilt was magnified by loss. When I stayed with my cousin as she said goodbye to her husband in hospice, I felt the weight of being there when his time ran out while I had been spared. I watched as life drained from his body, as the hands that once held so much love and strength grew still. The air in that room was thick with sorrow, with love, with an aching finality. And years later, when I was the only one in the room with my Nana as she took her last breath, the same questions returned. *Why was I still here?* I had survived a crash that should have killed me, yet I sat

THIS TOO SHALL PASS:
A Memoir of Survival, Loss, and Finding Purpose

in the presence of death time and time again, helpless to stop it.

There was a moment in those losses—staring at my cousin's hollowed expression, gripping my Nana's cooling hand—where I felt the weight of it all crash into me. The grief, the guilt, the unbearable silence of those who were no longer here. And in that silence, I heard the echo of my grandfather's words, the ones that had found me in the wreckage of my car when I was trapped and waiting for rescue: *This too shall pass.*

In time, I came to understand that my survival was not a mistake to atone for but a chance to live meaningfully. Instead of asking *Why did I survive?*, I began asking *What can I do with this life I've been given?* My healing became an offering—not just for myself, but to those who were no longer here to keep living their stories.

Survivors' guilt can be a paralyzing weight, keeping us tethered to the past and questioning our right to happiness. But when we carry it differently—when we allow it to shape our purpose rather than define our suffering—it becomes a source of strength. I began to realize that honoring those I had lost did not mean shrinking into sorrow but expanding into life. We do not honor the departed by living in the shadows of guilt but by embracing life with the fullness they were denied. We carry them with us in every moment we choose to truly live, in every breath we refuse to waste.

Survival is not just about existing. It is about learning to stand again, even on unsteady legs. It is about finding purpose in the pain, meaning in the moments of quiet. It is about knowing that while the ghosts of the past may always walk beside me, they are not here to haunt me. They are here to remind me that life is fragile, fleeting, and beautiful—and that it is not enough to survive. I must live.

THIS TOO SHALL PASS:
A Memoir of Survival, Loss, and Finding Purpose

CHAPTER 2:
WHO I WAS

I was born into a lively, tight-knit family that valued resilience, humor, and an unwavering sense of support. My parents worked tirelessly to provide a stable home for my four siblings and me, teaching us the importance of perseverance, kindness, and integrity. Our house was always bustling with activity—whether it was my older brothers roughhousing, pretending to be WWF superstars, my younger sister and brother screaming "Marco Polo" at the top of their lungs in the pool, or the uncontrollable laughter at the dinner table sparked by my father's relentless attempts to entertain five energetic kids while my mother tried to enjoy a rare moment of peace.

Despite the chaos, there was a sense of safety and love within those walls, something I would later learn not to take for granted. At the time, I didn't fully appreciate what it meant to grow up in a home filled with love, but as I got older, I realized that not everyone was fortunate enough to have that foundation. My childhood, though loud and unpredictable, was filled with warmth and connection.

One of my fondest memories from childhood was the endless summer nights playing manhunt with all the kids in the neighborhood. Our house was the central location, and the large oak tree in the front was our sacred "home base." Those nights held a kind of magic— running barefoot through dewy grass, the sound of cicadas humming in the background, and the exhilaration of hiding in the shadows, heart pounding, as someone counted down before the chase began. We could play outside long after the sun had set, safe in the unspoken trust we had in our neighbors and each other. It was the kind of freedom that, in hindsight, feels like a relic of a different time.

But childhood wasn't just games and laughter. It was also the space where I began to form my sense of self, even when self-doubt tried to creep in. From a young age, I had a wild imagination. I would create intricate stories in my head, acting them out with dolls or sketching scenes in my notebooks. Art, music, and storytelling became my sanctuaries. I could spend hours sketching fashion croquis, singing along to the music blaring from my father's hi-fi stereo, or writing poetry in the margins of my school notebooks. These creative escapes were not just hobbies—they were my way of making sense of the world, of expressing emotions I couldn't quite articulate yet.

Yet, I wasn't the naturally gifted child. Everything I achieved required tireless effort. Whether it was academics or art, I put in the extra hours, pushing myself to prove that I could succeed. I had big dreams—maybe I'd become an artist, a costume designer, or even a lawyer. No matter what, I knew I wanted to bring ideas to life, to create something that lasted beyond me.

Like most teenagers, I struggled with self-doubt. High school was a rollercoaster of achievement and insecurity. I pushed myself to meet expectations while simultaneously trying to figure out who I was. I juggled extracurricular activities, part-time jobs, and the weight of being a perfectionist. The pressure I placed on myself was relentless.

I wanted to be excellent, to prove that I was capable, but in doing so, I often neglected the softer parts of myself—the parts that needed rest, patience, and self-compassion.

When I got accepted into the Fashion Institute of Technology, everything seemed to fall into place. College was the place where I finally started to find my footing. I immersed myself in my major, Textile and Surface Design, and for the first time, I felt like I was exactly where I was meant to be. The demanding coursework, the hours spent in design studios, and the relentless push to create—it all energized me. I thrived in the fast-paced, high-pressure environment of New York City, balancing multiple jobs and a heavy workload while trying to carve out a future that felt authentic to me.

By the time I entered my mid-twenties, I thought I had finally made it. I had landed a career that allowed me to be both creative and independent. I was engaged to the love of my life, planning a wedding that would mark the beginning of a new chapter. Everything I had worked for was coming together. The sacrifices, the long nights, the self- doubt—they had all led me here.

But life has a way of taking unexpected turns.

Eight months later, everything would be thrown into a tailspin. Not by my own doing, not by some gradual unraveling, but by one person's poor decision. One moment of impact that would shatter the life I had so carefully built.

At the time, I had no idea what was coming. All I knew was that 2013 was supposed to be my year—the year everything fell into place. Little did I know that it would be the year my world would fall apart.

CHAPTER 3:
THE CRASH – A MOMENT BETWEEN WORLDS

The sun hung high in the sky, pouring its golden light onto the asphalt as I cruised along the Southern State Parkway. The day was perfect, the kind that whispered promises of ordinary joy. The hum of my Kia Soul's engine beneath me was steady, reassuring, as music filled the space around me. Avicii's *Wake Me Up* pulsed through the speakers, each beat syncing with the rhythm of the road, a soundtrack to my life in motion. The air conditioning cooled my skin, and I felt the warmth of the sun kissing the tops of my hands on the wheel.

I was in my own little world, my mind half on the road, half drifting between weekend plans and the mundane details of the day. A meeting later, a lunch date with my cousin, maybe a stop at the beach if time allowed. The kind of day that would be easily forgotten in the grand scheme of things. A moment in between moments.

Everything was normal. Until it wasn't.

Up ahead, a silver Camaro sat idle on the shoulder, its

blinker flickering like an unanswered question. Instinctually, I eased into the middle lane, giving it space. A subtle feeling stirred in my gut, something unspoken, a small warning that told me to stay aware. The kind of intuition you don't fully understand until later. I barely registered my reflection in the rearview mirror before everything changed.

The Camaro didn't turn onto the exit. It didn't hesitate. It lunged.

Time dilated, stretching out each second into something liquid and surreal. The world shifted into unbearable clarity. I saw the Camaro swerve across the grass, its tires spitting gravel as it shot onto the highway. I saw the briefest glimpse of its driver's silhouette before the impact came—a thunderous collision that reverberated through every fiber of my being.

The force hit me like a giant's fist. My Kia Soul jerked violently, tires screaming as it spun. The outside world blurred into a streak of colors—sky, pavement, trees, sky again—until there was no up, no down, only motion and sound and the sickening certainty that this was it.

Then—weightlessness.

I was airborne. Suspended between earth and sky, between past and future. The sensation was eerily calm, like floating in the deep end of a pool just before sinking under. And then the ground reached up to reclaim me. My car landed with a jarring force, skidding to a halt, its frame groaning in protest.

Silence.

The chaos had stopped, but the world hadn't returned. I was still here. But everything was... different.

I inhaled, but the air felt thick, metallic. My ears rang. The radio still played, but the song was distant, like hearing music through water. Pain bloomed through my body in waves, but it was a secondary sensation, background noise to something far more profound.

A presence.

I wasn't alone.

The darkness that had swallowed me wasn't empty. It was full, thick with something unnamable yet familiar. And then, I saw him.

My grandfather stood before me, looking as real as he ever had in life. He was younger, sharper, dressed in a suit that made him look like he had stepped out of time itself. His gold pinky ring caught the light, and an unlit cigar rested between his fingers. The smell of his aftershave—warm, earthy—wrapped around me like a childhood memory come to life.

"Speedy Bee," he said, his voice rich with affection. No one else had ever called me that. Just him.

I felt no fear, no pain. Only warmth. Only love. He wasn't shocked to see me. He wasn't sad. He was... expectant, as if he'd been waiting for me. I wanted to reach out, to step closer, but I couldn't move. Or maybe I didn't need to.

He smiled, his presence a balm against everything I had just endured. "This too shall pass."

And just like that, he was gone.

The world crashed back into existence. The weight of my body pressed into the seat, the sharp bite of metal and shattered glass in the air. The blare of sirens cut through the stillness, voices urgent and scattered. Something heavy was on my chest, but I was breathing. I was alive.

A voice, muffled but distinct, called from outside the wreckage.

"She's awake!"

The next moments blurred into a frantic symphony of movement. A retired NYPD officer, an off-duty EMT, and a social worker appeared, their hands and voices grounding me in reality. Panic flared when I realized I couldn't feel my legs. The jaws of life screamed as they tore through metal, the sound raw and terrifying, yet I found myself floating between two worlds—the one where my body was trapped in the wreckage and the one where my Pop's words still lingered.

At the hospital, the revolving door of visitors began. Nurses, doctors, and family, all coming to check on me, their faces shifting in and out of my haze of pain and medication. And then, there was Kenny. The concern on his face was a weight heavier than the crash itself, his hands hovering just over mine as if afraid they might break. His eyes, red-rimmed, searched mine for reassurance I didn't have to give.

I reached for my phone, my fingers trembling, and dialed my mother. She was 1,300 miles away, and my first words were a breathless, "The car's total."

A beat of silence. Then, her voice, laced with worry so deep I could feel it through the phone. "Cars can be replaced, but you can't."

The weight of that truth settled in my chest. But all I could focus on was how late I was for lunch. "I need to call my cousin. I was supposed to meet her. She's going to wonder where I am."

Kenny's grip on my hand tightened. "Loretta, you're in the hospital. Lunch can wait."

But my mind refused to process the enormity of what had happened. I was fixated on schedules, on obligations, on normalcy. As if, by holding onto those things, I could erase the trauma. As if I could convince myself that life hadn't just changed forever.

Doctors came and went, their words blurring together—concussions, contusions, tests, scans. I nodded, answered when I could, let them poke and prod, but I was still stuck in that moment before impact, still hearing my Pop's voice, still wondering if I had really come back alone.

THIS TOO SHALL PASS:
A Memoir of Survival, Loss, and Finding Purpose

This, too, shall pass.

I had survived. But something inside me had shifted, something irreversible. I wasn't the same person who had started that drive. I had left something behind on that stretch of highway.

And now, I had to figure out how to live with what remained. I never could have imagined the countless tests, doctor's appointments, or prescriptions that were in my future.

I expected the bruises to fade, the headaches to lessen, the stiffness to ease with time. But years after the accident, something still felt... off. My body ached in ways I couldn't explain, joints swelling unexpectedly, seizures would come and go, fevers appearing without reason. Doctors chalked it up to trauma, my body still recovering from the impact. I wanted to believe them. I wanted to believe that this was temporary.

But over time, my neurologist knew it was more than nerve damage from the accident and suggested I go to a rheumatologist. And with that, an entire new revelation began.

CHAPTER 4:
THE NATURE OF GRIEF

Grief is not a single moment, nor is it a process with a definitive end. It is a slow unraveling, an echo that reverberates through time. It reshapes who we are, forcing us to decide whether we will remain buried beneath its weight or rise through the wreckage.

Losing who I once was felt like mourning a death without a funeral. There were no condolences for the person I could no longer be. I learned to smile when people said, "You're lucky to be alive," even when my body felt like a prison. I nodded when they called me strong, even when all I wanted was permission to break.

At first, grief manifested as rage. I was angry at the driver who changed my life, at my body for failing me, and at the people who tried to comfort me but never truly understood. Later, the anger turned to silence—an emptiness that swallowed the light, leaving only the question of who I was supposed to be now.

No one teaches you how to grieve the version of yourself

that no longer exists. But I learned that grief, in all its brutality, is a teacher. It taught me that acceptance is not surrender. It is the acknowledgment that *this is what is*. And in that acknowledgment, healing begins—not as a return to who we were, but as a transformation into who we are becoming.

The loss of my former self was not the only grief I had to navigate. The people around me changed as well. Some friends drifted away, unable to handle the weight of my pain. Others stepped in unexpectedly, offering quiet companionship in moments when words felt unnecessary. Grief has a way of reshaping relationships, revealing who is willing to sit with us in the darkness.

Eventually, I came to understand that grief is not about letting go— it is about carrying differently. The past remains a part of us, but it does not have to define our future. We move forward not by forgetting but by weaving our losses into the fabric of who we are becoming.

CHAPTER 5:
THE EMOTIONAL TOLL OF TRAUMA

I remember that day with a vivid clarity that still haunts and inspires me—the moment the accident unfolded, time seemed to slow, each second etching itself into my memory like an indelible scar. In the weeks and months that followed, I found myself caught in a liminal space between who I once was and who I was forced to become, grappling with memories that felt both alien and intimately mine.

The accident wasn't just a single moment in time; it was the spark that set off a profound internal transformation. I still recall the overwhelming clamor of sounds, the disorienting blur of motion, and the tidal wave of emotions that swept over me, leaving me questioning the reliability of my own senses. In the aftermath, the familiar morphed into something strangely unsettling, as if a persistent fog had descended over my reality, blurring the line between past horrors and future anxieties.

The Uninvited Guest: Living with PTSD

Living with PTSD quickly became like hosting an uninvited, stubborn guest. Flashbacks would appear unannounced—a particular song, a sudden movement, or even the comforting aroma of freshly brewed coffee could catapult me back to that life-altering moment. It felt as though my mind had locked onto that day, replaying it in an endless loop, while anxiety crept into every corner of my existence, demanding attention with a persistence that was both maddening and oddly familiar. There were nights when sleep became an elusive friend, replaced by the relentless replay of memories that refused to be silenced. In those quiet, agonizing hours, I wrestled with the question of whether this enduring pain was a form of punishment or perhaps a message urging me to reevaluate what truly mattered in life.

Over time, I came to see these scars not as symbols of weakness but as badges of a hard-won resilience—a testament to the strength forged in the crucible of my own experiences.

The Aftermath: Adjusting to a New Reality

Adjusting to life after the accident felt like trying to navigate a city with ever-changing streets, where each step brought both uncertainty and a spark of unexpected clarity. Social encounters, once taken for granted, morphed into delicate balancing acts where every conversation held the potential to trigger a cascade of memories. Yet, amidst the chaos, I discovered moments of reprieve – a deep breath here, a shared laugh there—that reminded me I was still capable of joy.

I learned to lean into practices like mindfulness, creative expression, and the unwavering support of those who truly understood me.

Sometimes, I even found humor in the absurdity of it all, quipping that my heart had become the most unreliable co-pilot on this unpredictable journey. At first, every interaction felt like a test—a measure of how much I could withstand before retreating into the safety of solitude. But isolation, while tempting, only fed the cycle of fear and avoidance.

The most difficult part was reclaiming my sense of self. Before the accident, I was confident, independent, and full of dreams and ambitions. After the accident, I felt like a fragmented version of my former self. My physical body had survived, but mentally and emotionally, I was drowning in a sea of uncertainty. Who was I now? And would I ever feel like "me" again?

The Mind-Body Betrayal

I used to think my body and mind were on the same team— partners in navigating life's challenges. But after the accident, it felt like my body had turned against me. The once-simple act of standing, of moving, of trusting that my legs would carry me safely from one place to another, suddenly felt like a gamble. I resented the physical pain, the unrelenting fatigue, the sensation that I was walking through life wearing a heavy, invisible weight.

And then there was the hypervigilance, the unshakable

feeling that danger lurked around every corner. The sound of a car engine revving too loudly could send my heart racing. A sudden jolt of movement in my peripheral vision would make me tense as if bracing for impact. It was exhausting, living in a body that constantly anticipated disaster.

But the most insidious part of it all was the self-doubt. I began questioning my reality. Was I overreacting? Was I being weak? Should I be "better" by now? I wanted to rationalize my pain, but trauma doesn't adhere to logic. It lingers, waiting for the right trigger to remind you that it's still there.

Breaking the Silence: Therapy and Healing

For a long time, I hesitated to seek help. There was a part of me that believed I could handle it on my own, that if I just ignored it, it would go away. But PTSD is not something you can will into silence. It demands to be acknowledged.

Therapy became both a refuge and a battlefield. Some sessions left me emotionally drained, peeling back layers of buried fear and grief. Others provided glimmers of hope, small but significant victories that reassured me I wasn't beyond repair.

One of the most profound moments in therapy came when I realized that healing wasn't about erasing the trauma—it was about integrating it into my story. I had spent so much time resisting, wishing I could rewind the clock and undo what had happened, that I hadn't considered the possibility of moving forward despite it.

I learned coping mechanisms—breathing exercises for when anxiety surged like a rogue wave, grounding techniques for when I felt myself slipping into a memory, reframing thoughts that told me I was broken beyond repair. Bit by bit, I was rewriting the narrative in my mind. I wasn't a victim. I wasn't a prisoner of my past. I was a survivor.

Rebuilding Trust in Life

One of the hardest things to reclaim after trauma is trust—trust in others, in the world, in oneself. The accident had shattered my illusion of safety. Before, I moved through life with a quiet certainty that things would work out. Afterward, everything felt like a calculated risk. I found myself constantly bracing for the next disaster, unable to believe that good things could happen without a hidden cost.

It took time, but slowly, I began to find trust in the small things again. Trust in a morning routine that brought stability. I trusted in the kindness of loved ones who showed up, day after day, even when I felt unlovable. Trust in my strength, in the fact that I had already survived what I thought would break me.

The Art of Healing: Finding Myself Again

Art had always been my sanctuary, my way of making sense of the world. But after the accident, even that felt foreign to me. My hands, once so steady, would tremble. My focus would waver. I found myself staring at blank canvases, afraid to start, afraid that whatever I created would be tainted by the trauma I carried.

But one day, I picked up a paintbrush. Not because I felt ready but because I needed to. The first strokes were hesitant, uncertain. But as I let the colors spill onto the canvas, something inside me shifted. The pain, the fear, the grief—it all poured out, not in words, but in movement, in texture, in raw emotion.

Creating again didn't erase what had happened, but it gave me a language to express what words couldn't. It reminded me that I was still here. That I still had something to offer. That even in brokenness, there was beauty.

Moving Forward, One Step at a Time

Healing is not a straight path. It is not a destination you arrive at with certainty. It is a series of choices made every day—to get out of bed, to take another step, to keep going even when it feels impossible.

I won't say that I'm "over" what happened because trauma doesn't simply disappear. But I've learned that it doesn't have to control me. I've learned that I am more than the worst thing that ever happened to me. And most importantly, I've learned that healing is not about returning to who I was before—it's about becoming someone new, someone stronger, someone who carries the past but is not defined by it.

And so, I move forward—not unscathed, not unchanged, but still here. And that, I think, is enough.

Another Plot Twist

I told myself that my body was just adjusting, that the lingering stiffness and fatigue were normal after everything I had been through. But deep down, I knew something wasn't right. The pain wasn't just from the accident. My hands would swell so much that I couldn't grip a pencil, my legs would give out from underneath me some days, and exhaustion would hit me in waves so strong that even standing felt impossible. I convinced myself it was just stress, just trauma, just something else I had to push through.

Then one day, I pushed too hard. In February 2020, while in my office in New York City, I began to feel light-headed, my vision blurred, and I began convulsing. It was a day filled with meetings and deadlines, but this day, it all hit differently. I landed on the floor of my office, where I remained for what felt like an eternity. That was the last day I would be in that office. Not only was the world about to shut down due to a global pandemic, but my body had finally had enough. Another journey was about to begin. One that would leave all I had worked for behind me.

After meeting with my neurologist a few days later, they suggested I go to a rheumatologist to figure out that constant

pain, the swelling, and the fatigue. Once again, I was poked and prodded. I watched vial after vial of blood being drawn. In a few weeks, I had an answer.

Cryopyrin Associated Periodic Syndrome. Something that was always lying dormant but came to the surface due to the trauma of the crash years earlier.

CHAPTER 6
THE BURDEN OF SURVIVOR'S GUILT

The Weight of Survival

Survivor's guilt is an insidious emotion. It doesn't arrive in a single moment, nor does it make itself obvious at first. It creeps in, lingers in the quiet spaces, and settles into your bones when you least expect it. It whispers questions that have no answers: Why me? Why did I survive? Why was I spared when others weren't?

For me, survivor's guilt wasn't just a passing thought after the accident. It became a constant companion, a heavy weight I carried through every stage of my recovery. The feeling of being alive when others were not, of walking away from an accident that could have ended differently, haunted me in ways I didn't have words for at the time.

At first, I thought the guilt would fade as I healed. That once I regained my strength and found a new rhythm, the weight of it would lessen. But guilt doesn't work that way. Instead of dissipating, it deepened as time went on. The further I moved from that day, the more it felt like I was leaving something—or someone—behind.

Comparison: Was My Pain Enough?

After the crash, I found myself in a world of doctors, therapists, and recovery programs. My days were filled with physical therapy, with specialists monitoring my progress, with slow, incremental victories that should have been celebrated. But in those same spaces, I encountered people whose struggles seemed far greater than mine.

There were those who had lost limbs, those who were paralyzed, and those who would never walk again. I saw patients who had suffered severe brain injuries, their lives forever altered in ways I couldn't begin to comprehend. And then there was me—damaged but mobile, in pain but still functioning. My survival felt unfair in comparison to what others had lost.

I couldn't shake the thought: Did I even deserve to be here?

I had survived a crash that should have taken me, but I didn't lose the ability to walk. I wasn't in a coma. I hadn't spent months in the ICU. I had trauma, yes, but was it enough to justify the space I was taking in those hospital rooms, in those therapy sessions, in the world itself?

This self-doubt ate away at me, making it hard to acknowledge my own suffering. Instead of embracing healing, I diminished my own experience, convincing myself that my pain wasn't as valid as someone else's.

It wasn't until much later that I realized something crucial: Trauma is not a competition. Pain is not measured in degrees of suffering. Just because someone else has endured more does not mean that what I went through wasn't real, that it didn't shape me, or that it didn't deserve recognition. But in those early days, I wasn't ready to accept that.

The Guilt That Lingered

Survivor's guilt doesn't just come from living through an accident. It extends into every part of your life, reshaping the way you see the world. For me, it showed up in unexpected places.

It was in the moments of joy—when I laughed with friends, when I celebrated small wins, when I found peace in a sunrise. Guilt would seep in and remind me: You shouldn't be happy. You shouldn't be here. Someone else deserved this moment more than you.

It was in the quiet moments—when I lay awake at night, reliving the crash, remembering the peace I had felt in those seconds before impact. Maybe I wasn't supposed to come back.

And it was in the losses that followed.

Loss and the Cycle of Guilt

Grief moves at its own pace. It doesn't adhere to logic, nor does it wait for you to be ready. When Brian was diagnosed with cancer, it was as though time itself had turned against him, and against my cousin, his new bride. One moment, he was there—full of life, cracking jokes, making plans for the future—and then, without warning, the world began to slip away from him. The speed of it was dizzying, unrelenting.

I didn't even know he was sick until my cousin called me, her voice tight with something I couldn't yet name. "I need you," she said. There was no prelude, no softening of the blow, just those three words that carried the weight of a collapsing world. And in that moment, I knew.

I threw an overnight bag together, thinking I'd be back in a day or two. Seven days later, I would finally return home—though nothing would ever feel like home in quite the same way again.

The Unseen Shift

Looking back, I replay the last time I saw Brian before the diagnosis. It was at a wedding at the end of May, a bright summer day where everyone was laughing, dancing, and caught up in the celebration of love and new beginnings. He looked a little tired, maybe a bit quieter than usual, but nothing alarming. Nothing that prepared me for what would come just a few months later.

By November, he was in hospice. The in-between time barely registered. There was no slow descent, no gradual warning signs that allowed me to process what was happening. It was as if life had pressed fast forward, skipping entire chapters. One day, he was himself; the next, he was a shadow of the man I had gotten to know.

And then I was standing in the doorway of his hospice room.

A Sight for Sore Eyes

"Aren't you a sight for sore eyes."

Those were the first words he spoke when he saw me. His voice still held warmth, still carried something of the Brian I had always known.

But my heart sank. The man in front of me was not the man I had last seen. His body was frail, his skin stretched thin over bones that had once been strong. He had aged decades in the span of months. The vibrant 39-year-old who had once seemed invincible now looked as if he had lived another 50 years in the time we had been apart.

And yet, somehow, in that moment, we were still us. The weight of it all—the pain, the fear, the unspoken grief—hung in the air between us, but so did the friendship, the history, the laughter we had always shared.

I forced a small smirk, my voice light but trembling beneath the surface. "So this is how you get me to Connecticut, huh?"

For a split second, the spark of who he had always been flickered back to life. A quiet chuckle, a knowing glance. The joke landed, because of course, it did—that's how we had always handled life, with humor, even in the face of the impossible.

And then, silence.

Because the impossible was now real.

The next few days felt like a betrayal. These two people who were planning to spend the rest of their lives together were being short-changed. Their one-year wedding anniversary had just passed. But instead of celebrating with a bottle of rose, I was cutting up the smallest pieces of chicken parmigiana possible for him to swallow so he wouldn't choke.

The nights were filled with morphine-induced screams.

The days were filled with a rotating door of friends and family coming to say "goodbye".

In between the doctors, the nurses, and family, he and I got a lot of one-on-one time together.

Some of the hardest moments were when he was pleading with me to sneak him out of the facility and asking me what it was like to die.

Maybe when you are near death, you can see the ones who have also experienced it.

Maybe there's a certain glow to the ones that came back for the ones who are about to exit to cling to.

I wish I knew.

But laying on that cot, at 2:30 am, I would find myself quietly crying.

This wasn't a fair shake. I was here and someone who was incredibly loved was going. So much promise, so much hope, was lost before anyone could truly process it.

The Guilt That Follows

When someone you love is dying, no matter how present you are, no matter how much you give, there will always be a part of you that feels like it wasn't enough. That you should have done more, said more, been there sooner.

I found myself asking impossible questions. Why didn't I notice sooner? Why did I get more time and he didn't?

That's the thing about survivor's guilt—it doesn't follow reason. It latches onto the empty spaces, the what-ifs, the moments you can't go back and change. It convinces you that, somehow, you should have been able to stop the inevitable.

But grief is not a puzzle to be solved. It's a wound that never fully closes.

And so, I carry him with me—not just in the loss, but in the love. In the memories, in the echoes of his laughter, in the warmth of the moments we had. Even in the regret, there is gratitude. Because he was here. And for that, I am forever thankful.

Nana's Wisdom: The Privilege of Aging

Three years later, in November of 2022, I found myself in another room, watching another life slip away. This time, it was my Nana. She had been recovering from a broken hip, and while she was 99, she was still full of spirit. Just before she passed, we had been talking about lunch—she had hated the ravioli but enjoyed the cookie. It was such an ordinary conversation, so normal that I didn't see the shift coming.

And then, within minutes, she was gone. I was the only one in the room when it happened. The silence was overwhelming.

But Nana had always reminded me of something important— something she wanted me to carry with me after she was gone. "Aging is a privilege," she'd tell me. "Not all of us get the opportunity to do so."

She was the last of her generation. She had outlived everyone she ha d loved from her adolescence and early life. She knew the ache of loss intimately, yet she never let it harden her. She didn't want me to dwell on the fact that I was still here. She wanted me to enjoy every second of it—because I was lucky enough to experience it.

That thought lingers with me. The guilt of surviving still rises at times, but Nana's voice counters it. ***Aging is a privileg e***.

A lesson from someone who had seen nearly a century of life, who had learned what mattered in the end.

Finding Purpose in Survival

For a long time, I thought survivor's guilt meant I had to justify my existence. That I had to prove I was worthy of the life I had been given. But that mindset was exhausting. It kept me in a cycle of self- punishment, preventing me from truly living.

Eventually, I began to see my survival differently.

Instead of asking Why did I survive?, I started asking What can I do with this life I've been given?

I began volunteering and finding ways to give back. I sought out connections with people who had been through trauma, using my story to help others who felt lost in their own survival. I realized that the best way to honor the lives that had been lost was not to live in guilt but to live with purpose.

This shift didn't erase the guilt, but it gave it meaning. It allowed me to carry it differently—not as a weight that dragged me down, but as a reminder to live fully, to cherish the time I had been given, to use my experiences to support others.

Letting Go of the "Why"

I will never know why I survived that crash. I will never understand why I was spared while others have been taken too soon.

But maybe I don't need to know.

Maybe life isn't about answering the why. Maybe it's about choosing what we do with what remains.

So I choose to live—not to prove my worth, not to justify

my survival, but because life itself is a gift. Because even in grief and guilt, there is beauty to be found.

And because the best way to honor those we have lost is to keep moving forward, carrying their memory with us, living in a way that makes every borrowed moment count.

CHAPTER 7:
ASKING FOR HELP—STRENGTH IN VULNERABILITY

The Myth of Self-Sufficiency

There was a time in my life when I believed that asking for help was a sign of weakness. I had always prided myself on my independence, convinced that strength meant handling everything on my own. I thought that if I admitted I needed help, it would mean I had failed in some way— failed to be resilient, failed to be capable, failed to be the version of myself that I thought the world expected.

That belief carried over into every aspect of my life— work, relationships, and even my health. I was the person who always said, *I got this,* even when I clearly didn't. I carried my burdens silently, refusing to let anyone see the cracks in my armor. But the truth is that mindset nearly broke me.

When my life changed after the accident, I thought I could power through recovery the way I had powered through everything else in my life—on my own. But physical recovery is not just about getting back on your feet; it's about accepting that you may never walk the same path again. Emotional recovery is not just about moving forward; it's about allowing yourself to be supported along the way. For a long time, I resisted both.

Recovery wasn't just about regaining strength—it was about accepting that some things weren't getting better. I tried to push through the pain, to ignore the stiffness that made even simple movements feel impossible. I hated feeling weak. I hated needing help. But there were days when my joints ached so badly that I couldn't even grip my cane properly. My body, once something I could rely on, had become unpredictable, unreliable. And I had no idea why.

Breaking Point: When I Had No Choice but to Ask for Help

The turning point came when I could no longer deny that I needed support. After my traumatic brain injury in 2013, I found myself in a state of limbo—trapped between the life I had once known and the uncertainty of what lay ahead. In the immediate aftermath of the accident, I was in shock. I was physically stuck in my car for nearly an hour, but emotionally, I was stuck in a much deeper way.

Doctors assured me I would be fine, but I knew something was wrong. My body no longer felt like my own. I couldn't walk for a long time, and when I finally did, it felt like I was learning all over again. The simplest tasks—getting dressed, holding a brush, writing my name—felt foreign, like I was inhabiting someone else's body.

At first, I fought to push through on my own. I convinced myself that if I just tried hard enough, I could overcome it. I would sit in silence when my body ached, refusing to take the pain medication prescribed to me because I saw it as a crutch. I would pretend to be fine in front of family and friends, unwilling to acknowledge the struggle that raged beneath the surface.

But eventually, I hit a wall. The exhaustion, the frustration, the unbearable loneliness of suffering in silence—it all became too much. My body was screaming for rest, my mind was unraveling, and I realized that if I kept going like this, I would break.

And so, for the first time, I reached out.

The Power of Therapy: Learning to Accept Help

Making that first therapy appointment was one of the hardest things I've ever done. The stigma surrounding mental health had convinced me that needing therapy meant I was weak. But I was desperate—I needed someone to hear me, to see me, to help me untangle the mess in my head. Walking into that first session, I expected to feel ashamed. Instead, I felt relief. I had spent so long bottling up my pain, pretending I had everything under control, that I didn't realize how much I needed a safe space to let it all out.

Therapy didn't fix everything overnight. It was

uncomfortable at times, forcing me to confront things I had spent years avoiding. But it also gave me tools I never knew I needed. It helped me understand that vulnerability is not weakness; it is the foundation of healing. It taught me that asking for help doesn't mean you're incapable—it means you're human.

I learned that my reluctance to ask for help wasn't just about pride— it was about fear. Fear of being a burden. Fear of being judged. Fear of admitting that I wasn't as strong as I wanted to be. But through therapy, I started to see that true strength lies in knowing when to lean on others.

Relying on My Support System: The People Who Showed Up

When I finally allowed myself to ask for help, I saw just how many people were willing to give it.

My husband, Kenny, was there for me in ways I had never imagined. He was patient when I was frustrated, understanding when I was withdrawn, and steady when I felt like I was crumbling. He never made me feel like a burden, even when I felt like one.

There was a time in my recovery when I had to rely on a walker just to make it from room to room. When I left the house, I leaned on a cane. Some days, even that was too much—I was trapped on the couch, my body unwilling to cooperate with even the simplest tasks. Those were the worst days, when frustration burned hotter than the pain.

Kenny would step in, ready to help, but I met him with nothing but resistance.

"I got this!" I'd snap, my voice sharp with defiance. "I'm not a fucking cripple!"

He never flinched. He just stood there, patient as ever, his eyes steady, his hands at his sides like he was afraid to make the wrong move.

"I'm not saying you are," he'd say softly.

But I didn't hear him—not really. I was too busy fighting a battle he wasn't even part of. I wasn't angry at him. I was angry at myself, at my body, at the unfairness of it all. And in my rage, I lashed out at the one person who refused to walk away.

It took years—years of snapping, apologizing, and relearning how to let someone love me in my weakest moments—before I understood the truth. He didn't help me out of obligation. He did it because he loved me. Because watching me struggle hurt him, too.

And I finally realized that letting him in wasn't admitting defeat. It was allowing love to carry me when I couldn't carry myself.

My family showed up in ways I didn't expect. Some took longer than others, but eventually, we all found our way to the place my parents had always hoped for—there for one another when it mattered most.

Justin understood the severity of my situation better than anyone. As a paramedic with over a decade of experience, he saw firsthand what could happen to people who had been through what I had. He knew the long road ahead, the complications, the battles I'd face. He didn't need an explanation—he just got it.

My parents, though, struggled. They had always been my biggest supporters, but how do you support a child whose world has been shattered when you're 1,300 miles away? I only showed them what I wanted them to see. The thought of burdening them with the raw truth—how hard it was, how much I was struggling—felt selfish. They weren't around the corner, couldn't just drop by to check in, and I didn't want them losing sleep over something they had no control over. So, I filtered my reality, letting them believe I was doing better than I was.

My siblings gave me something invaluable—the gift of normalcy. Even on my worst days, they found ways to make me laugh. Justin would crack a joke at the most inappropriate moments, John would tease me like nothing had changed, Sal would remind me how stubborn I was, and Marie could always read me like an open book. In those moments, I wasn't the "injured" one. I was just their sister. But some days, it was hard.

There was a disconnect between me and some of my siblings—the ones who didn't fully understand what I was going through, the ones who, in their frustration, kept asking, "Why aren't you better yet?" It took time. Everything takes time. There were arguments about treatments, about whether I was seeing the right doctors, about whether I was doing enough to get back to who I used to be. To them, it seemed like I should have recovered already. The idea that I was still struggling didn't fit into the way they had always known me—strong, independent, in control. At first, that lack of understanding drove a wedge between us.

But time has a way of softening edges. As we got older and as life threw its curveballs at each of us, we began to see each other differently. The distance—both physical and emotional—shortened. We realized that the arguments, the frustration, the fear, had always come from a place of love. They wanted me to be okay. I wanted them to believe me when I said I wasn't.

Being in a big family means the dynamics are always shifting. We are all different people with different lives and different ways of seeing the world. But when we slow down, when we take the time to really listen, that love—the one thing that never changes—comes through. And for that, I am grateful.

I also found unexpected support in my friends. Some drifted away after the accident, unsure of how to handle the new reality of my life. Maybe they didn't know what to say, or maybe they were afraid of seeing me in a way that didn't match the person they had always known. Either way, their absence was felt. But the ones who stayed— the ones who sat with me in my hardest moments, who didn't need me to pretend to be okay—became my lifeline. They weren't just friends anymore; they were anchors, keeping me tethered when I felt like I might float away.

That time in our lives—our late twenties, early thirties—was a season of transformation for all of us. It was filled with weddings, babies, new careers, cross-country moves—all the "normal" milestones that come with growing up. And inevitably, we began to drift apart—not because of anything we had done to one another, but because life was simply happening. The spontaneous nights out became fewer, text conversations stretched into weeks instead of hours, and some of us found ourselves in different states, different time zones, and different worlds.

But despite the distance, I always knew they were there.

Friendships in adulthood aren't about constant presence; they're about knowing, without question, that no matter how much time passes, you can pick up right where you left off. The ones who stay are gifts— they are the family you choose. Sometimes, that meant watching *Wine Shades* make an appearance at a backyard get-together, our laughter filling the night air, reckless and carefree. Sometimes, it was quieter— sitting on their back porches in the morning, sipping coffee in worn-out pajamas, letting comfortable silence say what words didn't need to. Other times, it was just a text in the middle of a chaotic day, something ridiculous, a meme so absurd it made me laugh out loud in the middle of a doctor's office. Those moments, no matter how small, got me through.

Because friendship isn't measured in grand gestures or constant communication—it's found in the people who remind you, in ways big and small, that you're never truly alone.

Opening myself up to help didn't just ease my recovery—it deepened my relationships. It showed me that true connection is built not in moments of strength but in moments of raw, unfiltered honesty.

The Lessons I Learned About Strength

Through this journey, I learned that strength is not about enduring alone. It is about knowing when to reach out, when to let others in, and when to accept that you don't have to do everything by yourself.

I learned that vulnerability is not something to be ashamed of. It is an act of courage.

I learned that people want to help—not out of pity, but out of love.

And I learned that healing is not just about physical recovery; it is about allowing yourself to be cared for, to be supported, to be seen.

Finding Purpose Through Helping Others

As I navigated my healing journey, I realized that the best way to honor the help I had received was to extend that same compassion to others.

I began volunteering, finding ways to support those who felt lost in their own struggles. Whether it was through community outreach, speaking openly about mental health, or simply being there for a friend in need, I discovered that giving help was just as powerful as receiving it. There is something profoundly healing about turning pain into purpose. About using your own experiences to remind others that they are not alone.

That is what asking for help taught me—not just how to receive but how to give.

Final Thoughts: The Strength in Surrender

If there is one thing I hope others take from my journey, it is this: Asking for help is not a sign of failure. It is a sign of resilience.

We are not meant to navigate life alone. We are not meant to suffer in silence.

True strength lies in knowing when to say, *I can't do this by myself.*

And when you do, you will be amazed at how many hands reach out to lift you up.

So, if you are struggling, if you are carrying the weight of your pain alone, please—ask for help. There is strength in vulnerability. There is power in connection.

And most importantly, you are never as alone as you think you are.

CHAPTER 8:
HEALING AS A CHOICE

Healing is not a straight path. It does not come with a roadmap or a clear destination. It twists and turns, doubles back, and sometimes feels as though it has abandoned us entirely. It is not a singular moment of realization, nor is it a finish line we cross with certainty.

Healing is a choice—one we make every single day.

For a long time, I resisted that choice. I clung to my grief as if letting go of it meant betraying the person I used to be. I convinced myself that if I stopped mourning, I would be erasing the weight of my experiences, invalidating the love and loss that shaped me. But I have learned that healing does not mean forgetting. It does not mean moving on as if nothing happened. Instead, it is about learning how to carry the past differently, how to make space for sorrow without allowing it to consume everything else.

Just as I had begun to accept my body's limitations

post-accident, another unexpected twist arrived. In March of 2020, after years of unexplained pain, swelling, and fatigue, I was diagnosed with Cryopyrin- Associated Periodic Syndrome (CAPS), a rare autoinflammatory condition. The news was both a relief and a heartbreak. A relief, because, finally, there was an explanation. A heartbreak because it wasn't something that could be 'fixed.' It was now a part of me, just as much as my accident, just as much as my scars.

I had spent years convincing myself that if I worked hard enough, I could get back to who I used to be. But, CAPS forced me to let go of that illusion. It wasn't about 'returning' anymore—it was about adapting. About learning to respect my body instead of fighting against it. About finding new ways to create, new ways to live, without resentment. Healing wasn't just about overcoming—it was about learning how to exist within the reality of what is.

Art became my refuge when words failed me. When my hands, weakened by my diagnosis, could no longer hold a brush the way they once had, I adapted. I found new ways to create—through palette knives, through the pressure of my fingertips, through unconventional tools that allowed me to keep expressing what was too vast and too painful to say aloud. Art did not erase my grief, but it gave it form. It allowed me to release it onto canvas, to shape it into something tangible, something I could stand back and witness rather than let it devour me from the inside. Healing is not about returning to who we were before our tragedies.

That version of us no longer exists in the way we once knew. And that is not a loss—it is an evolution. Healing is about becoming someone new, someone who carries their scars with both sorrow and strength. It is about finding joy in unexpected places, in moments we once thought were lost to us. It is about embracing the unknown, not because we have no other choice, but because we choose to live—not as an obligation, but as an act of defiance, an act of hope.

Survival is not about proving our worthiness to exist. It is not about measuring our pain against someone else's or justifying why we deserve happiness after everything we have endured. Survival is about making every borrowed moment count, about choosing to keep going, even when the weight of loss presses down with relentless force.

Healing, I have come to understand, is not a singular destination— it is a lifelong practice of choosing ourselves, again and again. It is about showing up for ourselves, even when it is hard. Even when the wounds feel raw, even when the scars feel heavy. It is about rewriting the narrative, not to erase what we have been through, but to make room for hope, for growth, for the possibility of something beautiful emerging from the wreckage.

Some days, healing feels impossible. Some days, the past demands to be felt with an intensity that knocks the air from our lungs. But every step forward, no matter how small, is a step toward reclaiming ourselves. And that, I believe, is the most powerful act of resilience— choosing to live, to love, to create, despite it all.

CHAPTER 9:
A NEW DIAGNOSIS, A NEW REALITY

The Years of Not Knowing

When the light bulb finally flickers on, everything suddenly makes sense. For years, I was trapped in the dark, stumbling through symptoms that never seemed to connect—until someone finally flipped the switch. The signs had always been there, hiding in plain sight. As a child, I dealt with stiff joints, which were dismissed as "growing pains." The headaches and stomachaches? Just me being "an anxious child." The constant fevers and fatigue? With five school-aged kids under one roof, it was chalked up to me always catching some new bug. But it wasn't that. It was something more.

For most of my life, I didn't question it. I adapted. I thought this was just how my body worked—temperamental, unpredictable, weak in ways I could never explain. Even after the accident, when my body refused to heal in the way I was promised it would, I still convinced myself that this was normal.

I just needed more time.

The Diagnosis

By February 2020, almost seven years had passed since the crash, yet my body still felt like a battlefield. This wasn't just a "getting older" type of pain—this was debilitating. My joints stiffened until I felt like I was made of stone. My steps became clumsy and uncertain. Then, one day at work in New York City, my body betrayed me in a way I couldn't ignore—a pseudo-seizure that left me disoriented and terrified.

That was my breaking point. I needed answers.

After countless tests and appointments with neurologists who were just as confused as I was, one finally admitted, *"This can't be from the accident."*

But if it wasn't, then what the hell was it?

Eventually, I was referred to a rheumatologist, Dr. Tan. I didn't have high expectations—I had been let down too many times before. But the moment he walked into the room, something shifted.

He listened. Not just in the way doctors do when they're looking for a quick diagnosis to move on to their next patient. He asked questions, really asked questions, trying to connect the dots in a way no one else had before.

Then, he asked, *"Are you okay with getting some blood work done?"*

I almost laughed. Was I okay with it? After everything I had been through—my back nerves electrocuted and burned for pain management, EEGs that left permanent scars on my scalp, nerve tests that felt like torture devices—a simple blood draw was nothing.

I walked into the lab thinking they'd take a few vials. Instead, I watched as the technician lined up over a dozen.

"That's a lot," I said with a nervous chuckle.

The nurse just smiled. "You look like you can handle it."

She was right, and I was.

The Appointment That Changed Everything

Weeks later, I sat in Dr. Tan's office, waiting. The same dull exhaustion hung over me, the same unshakable doubt. Would this be just another dead end?

Then, he walked in, my file in hand.

"We found something in your genetic testing."

Three words that sent a shockwave through my system.

"Cryopyrin-Associated Periodic Syndrome—CAPS."

My mind blanked.

For a moment, I just sat there. Staring. The letters swam in my vision.

Dr Tan continued. *"You have a mutation of the*

NLRP3 gene." "Mutation?"

I thought, *"Why can't I get a cool superpower like in the comics!?"* *"Your body is overproducing a protein, 1L-1β…"*

A part of me felt relief. I wasn't crazy. My body hadn't been betraying me for no reason. There was something real, something in writing. A reason.

But then, the other shoe dropped.

"CAPS is a rare autoinflammatory disease. You've had it your entire life. It happens at the moment of conception."

My stomach twisted.

The headaches. The swelling. The fevers. The hearing loss in my left ear that I thought was from the accident. No. It had been CAPS all along.

"So what now?" I asked. "What are my options?"

Dr. Tan sighed. *"There's no cure for CAPS."*

And just like that, the ground beneath me shifted.

I had spent years convincing myself that one day, I'd get better. That all of this was just a long, painful recovery. But now, I had to face a new truth: this wasn't something I was going to heal from. This was something I would have to live with.

"There are treatments," Dr. Tan continued, *"but we won't know what works until we try them."*

And so began four and a half years of trial and error. Pills. Daily shots. Weekly injections. Monthly infusions. A science experiment with my body as the test subject.

Each attempt was a new form of hope—and each failure was a new kind of heartbreak.

The Reactions from People Around Me

That night, when Ken got home, I finally had an answer for him.

"Well, I'm one in a million!" I announced, throwing my arms up dramatically.

He blinked. *"What?"*

"Literally," I said, *"One in a million people get diagnosed with this. It's called Cryopyrin-Associated Periodic Syndrome—CAPS."*

Ken looked puzzled. *"Cryo-what?"*

I chuckled. *"Yeah, of course, I couldn't have something easy to say."*

As I explained it—how my white blood cells were attacking my joints, how my body was constantly inflamed, how every time I thought I was sick it was just a flare-up of this disease—I watched his expression shift. Not to fear. Not to pity. But to understand, it is a kind of relief.

For years, we had been stuck in a vicious cycle of unanswered questions, never knowing if what I was feeling was from the accident or something else entirely. Now, at least, we have an answer to some of the questions that have haunted us.

My parents were another story.

There was an unspoken rift between them over the diagnosis, and I'll never forget that FaceTime call.

My father scoffed, shaking his head. "Well, this is obviously from your mother's side."

I blinked. That was his first response?

On the screen, I watched my mother whip her head toward him, shooting him her famous side-eye—the kind that said, "It takes two to tango, buddy." I would have laughed if I wasn't so irritated.

Because really? That's what he chose to say? Not "Are you okay?" or "What happens next?" Just deflection—some odd form of his sarcastic humor, like he was trying to make a joke out of something that wasn't remotely funny.

For a moment, I just sat there, the silence stretching between us.

Maybe he didn't know what else to say. Maybe blaming genetics was easier than admitting the reality—that his daughter had lived with something her entire life, and they missed it. That every time I had been sick as a child, every unexplained fever, every ache, every doctor visit with no answers… was all connected.

I wasn't looking to blame anyone. But I think, deep down, my father didn't know how to process it. Maybe it was guilt.

Maybe it was just too big to grasp all at once.

And honestly? Neither did I.

Adapting to a New Reality

I always thought healing was something linear, You get hurt. You recover. You move on.

But CAPS shattered that illusion.

There was no "moving on." No magic cure. No checklist of treatments that would return me to the person I was before.

At first, I fought it. Hard. I pushed through the pain that left me gasping. I ignored the fatigue that crept into my bones like a slow, unrelenting tide. I convinced myself that if I just tried harder, just willed myself back into strength, I could beat this.

But you can't beat something that lives inside you. I had to learn a new kind of resilience.

I had to listen to my body instead of fighting against it. Treating it like an ally instead of an enemy. I had to stop seeing rest as a weakness and start seeing it as survival.

And I had to grieve. Not just for the body I once had but for the version of myself I thought I would be.

It took years. Years of trial and error, of medications that worked until they didn't, of treatments that promised hope but delivered more exhaustion. Years of learning how to exist inside this body, not despite it.

I had to find new ways to create—learning how to work with my hands when my joints refused to cooperate. New ways to exist, adjusting my space, my routines, my expectations.

New ways to live— without resentment. Without guilt. Without mourning the life I thought I'd have.

And one day, somewhere along the way, I stopped fighting to be the person I used to be—because I was finally learning to love the person I am now.

CHAPTER 10:
PROFESSIONAL PATIENT – NAVIGATING THE U.S. HEALTHCARE SYSTEM

The day I was diagnosed with Cryopyrin-Associated Periodic Syndrome (CAPS), I thought the hardest part was over. Finally, after years of unexplained pain, swelling, and exhaustion, I had an answer. I believed that now, with a name attached to my suffering, treatment would follow seamlessly, and I could focus on living rather than simply surviving.

I was wrong.

What no one tells you when you become chronically ill is that managing your health becomes a full-time job. A job with no benefits, no paid leave, and no option to quit. There are no training manuals or orientation days. You are simply thrown into the deep end, expected to navigate a labyrinth of insurance policies, medical jargon, endless paperwork, and an exhausting cycle of approvals and denials.

When people ask me what I do for a living, I often

half-jokingly say, "I'm a Professional Patient." Because that's what I am. Between fighting insurance companies for the medications my doctors insist I need, making calls to sort out billing errors, and scheduling appointments that always seem to be months away, managing my healthcare is an occupation all its own. The only problem is that it's one I never applied for.

The Insurance Gauntlet

The first time my insurance denied a prescription for my treatment, I was stunned. The doctor had prescribed it. I had a diagnosis. I was suffering. So why would they deny me the very medication meant to help?

The answer was buried in pages of fine print, hidden behind pre- authorizations, tiered pricing, and insurance codes that seemed purposefully designed to confuse. In their world, it wasn't about need— it was about cost. The insurance company wasn't looking at me as a person; I was just a case number, a financial equation to be solved in their favor.

What followed was an exhausting series of appeals, letters of medical necessity, and phone calls that all seemed to end the same way: *We will review your case and get back to you in 14 to 30 business days.*

Meanwhile, my body wasn't on pause. It was still in pain. The swelling in my joints didn't care about bureaucratic red tape. The fever and fatigue weren't interested in waiting for approval codes. But I had no choice.

Some medications, the ones that actually worked, came with price tags so astronomical that they may as well have been luxury cars. Five thousand dollars for a month's supply. Ten thousand. More. Some specialty medications cost close to $20,000 a month for ONE medication. And even with Medicare, another medication costs over $450 out of pocket. The numbers didn't even feel real. I would stare at invoices in disbelief, wondering who, exactly, could afford to stay alive in this system. Because it certainly wasn't me.

The Cost of Being Sick

Being disabled in America is expensive. Not just in dollars, but in time, in stress, in mental exhaustion. Every appointment, every prescription, every therapy session comes with a price—whether financial or emotional.

Even with insurance, copays stack up. A specialist visit might be $50 or $100 each time. Bloodwork, imaging, and other tests sneak in unexpected fees. And then there's the out-of-pocket maximum—the mythical number that, once reached, is supposed to mean insurance covers everything. The problem? It resets every year. Every January, it's like starting over, watching thousands of dollars drain from savings before real coverage even begins.

And if you need a treatment that isn't considered "mainstream enough", "cost-effective", or "medically necessary" (my personal favorite), by insurance standards? Good luck.

Many specialty medications are placed on what's called a "nonpreferred" tier, meaning insurance will cover little to nothing, even if it's the only thing that works for your condition.

So you're left with choices that don't feel like choices at all: Do I fight for another month's supply, knowing I may lose? Do I ration my medication, taking less than prescribed just to make it last? Or do I go without and hope for the best?

Paperwork, Phone Calls, and Learning the System

Nothing in this system is designed to be easy. The paperwork is never-ending. Forms for disability benefits, forms for medication approvals, forms for assistance programs, forms for financial aid. Some days, it feels like my full-time job is just filling out the same information over and over, sending it into a void, and hoping someone on the other side decides to process it before it "accidentally gets lost in the system."

And the phone calls. My God, the phone calls. If I had a dollar for every minute I've spent on hold, waiting for a faceless representative to tell me I need to call a different department, I could probably afford my own medication. The music alone could drive you absolutely insane. It is a twisted mix of elevator rock and classically infused techno. Painful enough to make even a harden spy crack and spill the beans.

I have learned the secret language of these conversations. Phrases like "I need to escalate this to a case manager" and "Can I speak to a supervisor?" have become my battle cries. I know which buttons to press to bypass the automated systems, how to frame my words so that my case gets flagged as urgent. I also learned the game of contacting pharmaceutical companies to see if they have programs to help cover the cost of my medications. Some companies offer financial assistance, providing medication at a reduced cost or even for free. But not all programs are accessible to me. Since I am on Medicare, I am often disqualified from these assistance programs. If I had private insurance, I would be eligible. The irony is infuriating. The very people who need the help the most are often the ones locked out of receiving it.

I have fought battles and won small victories. But each fight comes at a cost. The stress alone can trigger a flare-up, the very thing I'm fighting to prevent.

The Mental Toll of It All

The emotional weight of navigating this system is crushing. The stress, the constant advocacy, the feeling that you are always on the edge of losing access to the care you need—it all takes a toll.

Some days, I wonder if the exhaustion of fighting the system is worse than the illness itself. The feeling of being dehumanized, reduced to paperwork and policy numbers, wears on you. It chips away at your resolve. And the worst part? I know I'm not alone. I have met countless others in the same battle. Parents fighting for their children's treatments. Elderly patients trying to understand why their medications suddenly cost triple.

People forced to launch GoFundMe campaigns just to afford a basic necessity: staying alive.

Learning to Navigate, Learning to Survive

Over time, I have become an expert at navigating this system. I know which battles to fight and which to surrender. I've learned to keep meticulous records, to ask the right questions, to advocate for myself in ways I never thought I'd have to. But I am tired.

This is not how healthcare should be. It should not be a battlefield. It should not be a system designed to wear people down until they give up. But this is the reality we live in. And until it changes, I will keep fighting.

Because I have no other choice. Because I am a Professional Patient. And because my life—our lives—are worth the fight.

CHAPTER 11:
REBUILDING IDENTITY

The Fracture of Self

The hardest part of survival isn't the accident itself—it's what comes after. It's waking up in a body you no longer recognize, trying to make sense of a world that kept moving forward while you were stuck in place. It's staring at the ceiling late at night, wondering who you are now that everything has changed.

For weeks after the accident, I avoided mirrors. I didn't want to see the bruises, the scars, the reminders of how fragile my body had become. The person staring back at me wasn't the same woman who had walked into her car that morning, full of plans, full of expectations. She was a stranger, one with hollow eyes and a tentative, unsteady grip on life.

I wasn't sure how to exist in this new version of myself. The loss wasn't just physical—it was emotional, psychological. Who was I if I couldn't move the way I used to? What if I couldn't work the way I had before? What if I no longer fit into the world I had so carefully built for myself?

Trauma does more than shatter bones or leave bruises—it fractures identity. It forces you to mourn the person you once were while being thrust into the unknown, tasked with rebuilding from the ruins of who you used to be.

The Stages of Identity Grief

Much like the well-known five stages of grief, losing one's sense of self comes with its own cycle of mourning. I moved through these stages like an unpredictable tide, never in a straight line, often drowning in the weight of emotions I didn't yet understand.

Denial: This Isn't Who I Am

At first, I refused to acknowledge that my life had changed permanently. I told myself that if I worked hard enough, if I just *tried* harder, I could get back to who I was before the accident. I pushed my body beyond its limits, ignored my pain, convinced that healing was simply a matter of willpower.

When my body pushed back—when I collapsed in exhaustion or found myself unable to perform the simplest tasks—I spiraled into frustration. The disconnect between my mind and my physical reality was unbearable. I couldn't accept that this was my life now, that my body had betrayed me, that I couldn't just force my way back to the life I had lost.

Anger: Why Did This Happen to Me?

The anger was suffocating. It wasn't just directed at the driver who had changed my life in an instant—it was at the universe, at fate, at my own body. I raged at the injustice of it all. I had done everything right. I had worked hard, followed my dreams, and built a life that I was proud of. So why did this happen to *me?*

I lashed out in small ways, snapping at well-meaning friends who told me I was "so strong" when I felt anything but. I resented the doctors who couldn't fix me, who kept giving me vague answers and timelines that meant nothing. And worst of all, I was angry at *myself*— for not being stronger, for not healing faster, for not being the person I used to be.

Bargaining: If I Just Push Harder, Maybe...

I tried everything: new treatments, different therapies, and routines designed to "speed up" my recovery. I thought that if I just found the right solution, the right strategy, I could reclaim what had been lost.

I kept thinking, *If I just do this, maybe I'll feel like myself again.*

But I didn't. No amount of effort could undo the past. No miracle cure was going to give me my old body, my old life, my old self back. Coming to terms with that was one of the hardest realizations of all.

Depression: Who Am I Now?

The moment I stopped fighting reality, the weight of grief hit me like a tidal wave. I felt lost, disconnected from the world and myself. The things that used to bring me joy—art, movement, and even simple pleasures like listening to my favorite music—felt distant.

I didn't recognize the person I had become, and I wasn't sure I wanted to. Who was I if I wasn't the driven, ambitious, independent woman I had been before? What did I have to offer if my body could no longer keep up with the demands of my dreams?

For a long time, I existed in this space—adrift, uncertain, mourning the life I had lost but unable to see a future beyond it.

Acceptance: Becoming Someone New

Healing didn't come in a sudden, dramatic realization. It came in small, quiet moments—the first time I was able to stand a little longer without pain, the first time I created something new without comparing it to my past work, the first time I looked in the mirror and didn't hate the person staring back at me.

I slowly began to understand that rebuilding my identity wasn't about going *back* to who I was. It was about becoming someone new. Someone who had survived. Someone who had been broken and had found a way to put herself back together, piece by piece.

Redefining Strength

Before the accident, I thought strength meant independence. It meant pushing forward, handling everything on my own, and never asking for help. But after the accident, I learned a different kind of strength—the strength to be vulnerable, to accept help, to admit that I couldn't do this alone.

Strength wasn't in pretending I was fine; it was in acknowledging that I wasn't and still choosing to move forward anyway.

I had to rebuild not just my body but my identity. I had to accept that I wasn't the same person I had been before—and that wasn't necessarily a bad thing. The woman I was becoming was different, yes, but she was also resilient. She had faced the unimaginable and survived. She was learning, adapting, finding new ways to live, new ways to create, new ways to be whole.

Finding Joy in New Ways

One of the hardest parts of my recovery was accepting that some things would never be the same. Certain activities, certain movements, and certain expectations had to be adjusted. But rather than focus on what I had lost, I started to explore what I could still do.

I found joy in unexpected places—in slower mornings where I could appreciate the sunrise, in art that looked different from what I used to create but still carried meaning, in connections with people who understood what it was like to rebuild from the ground up. I learned that my worth wasn't tied to what I could physically do but to who I was as a person.

Embracing the Unknown

Rebuilding my identity wasn't about returning to who I had been before—it was about becoming someone new. It was about taking the pieces of my old life and weaving them into something different, something still beautiful, even if it wasn't what I had planned.

The truth is, life doesn't always go the way we expect it to. Sometimes, it takes unexpected turns, forcing us to grow in ways we never imagined. And while I wouldn't have chosen this path, I have learned to walk it with courage.

I am not just a person who survived a crash. I am the person who kept going, who adapted, who found new ways to live.

And in that, I found a strength I never knew existed.

This is my life now. And I am learning to embrace it.

CHAPTER 12:
FINDING HEALTHY OUTLETS – REDIRECTING ENERGY

The Uncontainable Energy of Trauma

In the aftermath of trauma, I discovered something I wasn't prepared for—a surge of restless, uncontainable energy. It wasn't the kind of energy that fueled excitement or joy, but rather a storm of emotions, a feeling of internal chaos that made it impossible to sit still. My mind was racing, my emotions fluctuating between grief, anger, and confusion, and my body felt like it was always on high alert.

At first, I didn't understand what was happening. I thought healing meant rest, stillness, and allowing my body to repair itself. But no matter how much I tried to slow down, my mind wouldn't let me. The emotional weight of the accident, the sudden loss of control over my body, and the daily struggle with pain created a whirlwind inside me. I needed an outlet—something to focus on, something to ground me. Over time, I learned that this energy didn't have to be something to fight against. Instead, I could transform it into something meaningful, redirecting it into healthier outlets that not only helped me cope but also began to shape a new version of myself.

The Power of Movement: A New Relationship with My Body

For someone whose body had been through trauma, movement was complicated. After the accident, I had to learn how to move again, how to trust my body despite the pain. I was afraid of doing too much, of pushing too hard, of making things worse.

But I also knew that staying still would only trap me in a cycle of fear and frustration. So, I started small.

At first, it was just stretching in bed, testing my range of motion. Then, I started going for short walks, just a few minutes at a time. At first, they felt like monumental tasks—every step was a reminder of what my body had endured. But as I kept going, something changed.

Walking became a ritual, a way of reconnecting with myself. It wasn't about physical fitness; it was about movement for the sake of feeling *alive*. The rhythm of my steps became meditative, grounding me in the present moment. Walking outside, breathing in fresh air, feeling the world move around me—it reminded me that I was still here. Still moving. Still fighting. The more I moved, the more I started to reclaim my body. I stopped seeing it as something broken and started seeing it as something resilient. Every step was an act of defiance against the limitations I had once feared.

Journaling: Writing My Way to Healing

Writing wasn't something I initially saw as a coping mechanism. It was just something I did when my thoughts became too overwhelming. At first, my journal was a mess of emotions—anger, grief, exhaustion, frustration. I wrote down things I didn't feel comfortable saying out loud. I let my words be messy, raw, and unfiltered. What I didn't realize at the time was that journaling was helping me make sense of my trauma. It allowed me to put words to feelings that had been too big, too tangled to process in my head. It gave me a way to track my progress, to see the small victories that often felt invisible in the day-to-day struggle.

Over time, journaling became more than just a venting space—it became a conversation with myself. I started writing about things I was grateful for, even on the hardest days. I wrote about my dreams, my hopes, and the lessons I was learning along the way.

One of the biggest realizations I had was that healing isn't linear. Some days felt like progress, and others felt like I was back at square one. But when I looked back at my journal entries, I could see the bigger picture. Even on the hardest days, I was still moving forward.

Journaling didn't erase the pain, but it gave me a way to

hold it, to understand it, to see it as part of my story rather than something that controlled me.

Creating Art: A Language Beyond Words

If there was one thing that truly saved me, it was art.

Before the accident, art had been my career, my passion, my way of expressing myself. After the accident, it became something even more powerful—it became my therapy.

At first, I was terrified that I wouldn't be able to create the way I used to. The pain in my hands made it difficult to hold a brush for long periods, and I felt like I was losing a part of myself. But instead of giving up, I adapted.

I started using different tools—palette knives, cake piping bags, anything that didn't require a tight grip. I experimented with new techniques, embracing textures and abstract forms in a way I never had before. And something incredible happened.

My art changed. It became more expressive, more raw, more *alive*. It wasn't just about creating something visually beautiful—it was about channeling my emotions onto the canvas. Every stroke, every color choice, and every texture was a reflection of what I was feeling inside.

I realized that my hands didn't have to move the way they used to for me to create. I could still make art. I could still tell my story. In doing so, I found a way to reclaim the part of myself I thought I had lost.

Music: The Soundtrack to Survival

Music had always been a part of my life, but after the accident, it took on a new significance. Certain songs became lifelines, pulling me out of dark moments, reminding me that I wasn't alone.

There were songs that made me cry, songs that gave me strength, and songs that made me feel seen. I started making playlists for different emotions—one for when I needed to feel strong, one for when I needed to let myself grieve, one for when I just needed to breathe.

There were days when words failed me, when I couldn't find a way to express what I was feeling. But music filled that space. It spoke the words I couldn't say, gave shape to emotions I didn't know how to process.

And in those moments, with my headphones on, eyes closed, feeling the rhythm pulse through me, I felt like I could exist beyond the pain.

Finding Joy in the Small Things

One of the hardest parts of my recovery was accepting that some things would never be the same. Certain activities, certain movements, and certain expectations had to be adjusted. But rather than focus on what I had lost, I started to explore what I could still do.

I found joy in unexpected places—in slower

mornings where I could appreciate the sunrise, in laughter shared with friends, in small victories that once felt impossible. I learned that my worth wasn't tied to what I could physically do but to who I was as a person.

Healing wasn't about going back to who I was before the accident. It was about becoming someone new. It was about taking the pieces of my old life and weaving them into something different, something still beautiful, even if it wasn't what I had planned.

The Art of Redirection

Trauma leaves you with energy that has nowhere to go. The pain, the anger, the grief—it all builds up inside, demanding to be acknowledged. I learned that I couldn't ignore it, but I could redirect it. Through movement, writing, art, music, and simple moments of joy, I found ways to transform my pain into something meaningful. I stopped fighting against the storm inside me and instead found ways to navigate it. In doing so, I discovered something unexpected. I wasn't just surviving. I was creating.

Creating a new way to live, a new way to heal, a new way to exist in a world that had once felt unrecognizable.

And in that, I found hope.

Because even after everything I had lost, I still had the power to build something beautiful.

And that, in itself, was worth everything.

CHAPTER 13:
THE SPIRITUAL SIDE OF HEALING

A Near-Death Experience That Changed Everything

Before my accident, spirituality was something I thought about in passing—something that lingered in the background, tied loosely to the traditions I was raised with, but never something I explored deeply. I had gone through the motions: Sunday Masses, prayers before meals, moments of gratitude whispered into the ether without much expectation of a response. Faith was something I acknowledged but never truly leaned on.

Then, in the span of a few seconds, I was thrown into a reality that left no room for skepticism. The accident didn't just have a physical impact; it was a fracture in the fabric of my existence, an opening into something I wasn't prepared to see but couldn't turn away from.

The moment before the crash, everything slowed down. I remember gripping the steering wheel, my heart hammering in my chest, my instincts screaming that something was wrong. The seconds stretched unnaturally long, as if time itself was bending. Then— impact. A violent, deafening collision. The sensation of weightlessness as my car lifted off the ground. The force pressed my body into my seatbelt, my limbs frozen in place.

And then, a void.

A deep blackness that wasn't empty at all—it was *full*. Full of silence, full of stillness, full of something I can only describe as presence. I wasn't afraid. There was no pain, no panic. Just… peace. An all-encompassing, absolute peace.

And then, I saw him.

A Grandfather's Visit from Beyond

He stood before me, looking as real as he ever had in life—except younger. Stronger. He wasn't the older man I had known as a child. This version of him was vibrant, full of life, and dressed in a tailored suit that made him look like he had stepped out of a 1940s film. His gold pinky ring glinted in the soft glow of whatever space we were in, and a cigar rested between his fingers, unlit.

"Speedy Bee," he said.

No one else had ever called me that. Just him. And at that moment, I knew.

I knew I had left my body. I knew I wasn't in that car anymore. I knew I was somewhere beyond the boundaries of the world I had always known.

My Pops didn't look sad or surprised to see me. He just smiled, that same gentle smile I had always associated with safety. He didn't say much—he didn't have to. I understood him perfectly, even without words.

"This, too, shall pass," he said.

It was what he always said when things got tough. When I was a kid and scraped my knee, when I had a bad day at school, when I doubted myself—those were always his words.

And then, just like that, he was gone.

The colors around me faded, and suddenly, I was back in my car, surrounded by flashing lights and strangers shouting for help. The weight of my injuries hit me all at once, but I barely registered the pain. My mind was still there, with him, trying to grasp what had just happened.

Coming Back Changed

I didn't tell anyone about what I had seen at first.

I wasn't sure how to put it into words. I wasn't even sure if it was *real*—at least, not in the way the physical world defines reality. But deep in my gut, I knew I hadn't imagined it. It hadn't been a hallucination. It had been something else entirely.

For months, I replayed that moment in my head, trying to make sense of it. If my grandfather had truly been there, what did that mean? Was it proof that there was something beyond this life? Was it a trick of my injured brain trying to comfort itself?

I wrestled with those questions in the stillness of recovery.

I had always thought spirituality was about having concrete answers— about believing in something because you were *supposed* to. But the accident changed that. It showed me that faith isn't about certainty. It's about *wonder*. It's about allowing yourself to *not* have all the answers and still choosing to believe in something bigger than yourself.

The Aftermath: A Shift in Perspective

After I was discharged from the hospital, I started seeing the world differently. Small things carried new weight: the way the sunlight hit my bedroom wall in the morning, the sound of the wind rustling through the trees, the way music could make me feel *alive* even when my body was broken.

Before, I had taken these things for granted. Now, I understand that life is made up of these fleeting moments, these tiny, often- overlooked gifts.

But the change wasn't just how I saw the world. It was how I *felt* within it.

I no longer feared death the way I once had. That's not to say I *wanted* to die—I fought every day to rebuild my life—but I knew, with an unshakable certainty, that there was more waiting for us beyond this existence. My grandfather's presence had made that clear.

But I also knew something else: I wasn't *supposed* to be

there yet.

I had been given a second chance. And if I had learned anything from my near-death experience, it was that I needed to make it count.

Redefining Spirituality

Before the accident, my relationship with faith had been complicated. I had grown up in the Catholic tradition, surrounded by rituals and prayers, but I had never felt truly connected to it. It always felt like something external, something I was expected to believe in rather than something I *felt*.

But after the accident, faith became something else entirely. It wasn't about rules or doctrines. It wasn't about reciting prayers because I was told to. It was about *connections*.

Connection to the universe.

Connection to the people I loved—both here and beyond.

Connection to the quiet moments where I felt something bigger than myself moving through the world.

I started exploring spirituality on my terms. I meditated. I spent time in nature, listening—not just to the sounds around me but to *myself*. I found comfort in music, in art, in the simple act of breathing deeply and knowing that I was *still here*.

Most of all, I started paying attention to the synchronicities, to the moments of unexplainable peace, to the way my grandfather's words would echo in my mind at exactly the right times.

"This too shall pass."

Healing as a Spiritual Journey

Healing, I learned, isn't just about physical recovery. It's about *acceptance*.

It's about recognizing that some things will never be the same and finding peace in that reality.

It's about trusting that even in the darkest moments, we are not alone. It's about understanding that our scars—both visible and invisible— are not signs of weakness but proof that we have *survived*.

And more than anything, it's about *choosing* to keep going, even when you don't have all the answers.

The Lesson That Stayed with Me

I don't know what happens after we leave this life. But I do know this: Love doesn't end.

The connection doesn't end. And we are never truly alone.

My grandfather didn't come to me that day just to say goodbye. He came to remind me that life is fleeting, but it is *not* meaningless. That even the hardest moments will pass. That I still had work to do here.

And so, I live.

Not perfectly. Not without pain. But with *purpose*.

THIS TOO SHALL PASS:
A Memoir of Survival, Loss, and Finding Purpose

Because this life—messy, unpredictable, heartbreaking as it is—*is a gift.* And I refuse to waste it.

CHAPTER 14:
RELATIONSHIPS AND RECOVERY

It's wild how one unexpected accident can flip your world upside down, reshuffling the people and relationships you thought you knew. One minute, you're cruising along, and the next, you're caught in a whirlwind where every bond is tested. Trauma doesn't just happen to you—it happens to everyone around you. It reveals truths you weren't prepared to face, shifts dynamics in ways you never imagined, and forces you to see people—yourself included—through an unfiltered lens.

I used to think that my relationships were built on unshakable ground. That the people I loved, the ones I relied on, would always be there. But trauma is a stress test. It doesn't just expose the cracks—it widens them. It makes the strong connections stronger and exposes the weak ones for what they are. It took me years to fully understand that and even longer to accept it.

Friendships: The Ones Who Stayed, the Ones Who Left

THIS TOO SHALL PASS:
A Memoir of Survival, Loss, and Finding Purpose

In the days following my accident, I quickly discovered which friends were as reliable as a pair of well-worn sneakers and which were more like those flashy new kicks that lose their shine after one wear. Some friends disappeared faster than ice cream on a scorching day, leaving behind a silence that spoke volumes.

I used to replay the moments when they pulled away, wondering if I had done something wrong. Maybe I was too much. Maybe my pain made them uncomfortable. Maybe they just didn't know how to show up for me. But then, I realized something that set me free: my trauma didn't *scare* them away. They just weren't meant to stay.

It's a hard lesson to learn, especially when you're already navigating loss. Some friendships, no matter how deeply rooted you thought they were, simply cannot withstand the weight of grief, uncertainty, and change. And that's okay. Not everyone is meant to walk through every chapter of your life. Some people are only there for a few pages.

And then there were the ones who showed up in ways I never expected.

These were the friends who didn't need me to explain what I needed—they just *knew*. They sat with me in silence when words felt useless. They sent texts, even when I didn't respond, just to remind me I wasn't alone. They showed up at my door with coffee, or food, or just themselves, willing to listen or simply *be* with me. They didn't try to fix me or tell me to "move on."

They honored my pain. They understood that healing is not a timeline—it's a process.

One of my closest friends told me something I'll never forget:

"You don't have to be okay for me to be here."

That sentence changed everything for me.

I had spent so much time feeling like a burden, like my pain was something that pushed people away. But real friends don't need you to be okay all the time. They don't leave when things get messy. They don't disappear when the light dims. They sit with you in the dark until you're ready to walk toward the light again.

Marriage: A Plot Twist I Never Saw Coming

I once pictured my wedding as a flawless fairy tale—a day filled with laughter, perfect timing, and a well-rehearsed "I do." Then, 28 days before our vows were set to be exchanged, life threw an accident my way that completely rewrote the script. It wasn't the romantic twist I'd envisioned; it was a harsh lesson in resilience and redefined priorities.

In those whirlwind 28 days, the pristine image of marriage I'd held evaporated, replaced by a raw, unfiltered reality. As I grappled with new challenges, my soon-to-be husband stepped in—not as a groom, but as my caregiver. Even before we were legally bound, he was there, tending to my needs and soothing my fears in doctors' visits and quiet recovery moments.

There were days when reconciling the man I thought I'd marry with the one guiding me through this recovery felt almost surreal. Yet, amidst the chaos, we found humor—in mispronounced medication names, disastrously botched attempts at making dinner, and shared laughs that lightened even the darkest moments.

This unplanned caregiving chapter reshaped our relationship. We learned to communicate on a deeper level, blending the roles of caregiver and partner into a bond uniquely our own. It wasn't the marriage I'd once envisioned, but it was one forged in the fires of adversity—a living testament to the transformative power of true commitment.

Marriage, I learned, isn't just about the good times—it's about the moments that test you, the moments that strip away the filters and reveal who you truly are. And in those moments, I saw the kind of love that doesn't waver, doesn't falter. The kind of love that stays. But it wasn't always easy.

There were days when the weight of my trauma felt too heavy for both of us. Days when I was frustrated and angry at the world, at my body, at the unfairness of it all. And sometimes, that anger spilled over onto the person who loved me most. It's hard to be vulnerable, even with the one person who sees every part of you. But love—real love— doesn't demand perfection. It allows space for the hard moments, for the days when you don't have the energy to pretend you're fine.

And that's what I learned in the hardest moments of my recovery: Love isn't found in the easy days. It's found in the ones where everything feels impossible, and yet, you still choose each other.

Family: Redrawing the Puzzle

Family is supposed to be your haven, but after the accident, I realized that even family relationships shift under the weight of trauma. Some grew stronger, while others became strained. The people who had always been there suddenly didn't know what to say, and the people I least expected to step up became my biggest sources of strength.

One of the most frustrating things about dealing with trauma is how others perceive it. Some family members, in their attempt to help, would say things like, *"At least you survived."* And while I knew they meant well, it made me want to scream. Because survival isn't just about being alive. It's about *living*. And in the early days of my recovery, I didn't feel like I was *living* at all.

Others didn't know how to talk about what had happened, so they avoided the topic altogether. And that hurt differently. It felt like they were erasing a part of my experience, like they wanted to pretend it hadn't happened because it was too uncomfortable for them to acknowledge. But then there were the moments of grace.

Like when my siblings, the ones who had always been my partners in crime, found ways to make me laugh even when I didn't want to. When my parents, despite not always knowing the right words, reminded me every day that I was still *me*—that I was still their daughter, still strong, still capable of rebuilding.

Family, I learned, is not just about blood. It's about the people who stay, who show up, who hold you when you're falling apart and remind you that *you are not alone*.

Recovery: A Winding Path of Growth

Recovery is rarely a straight line. It's a winding path filled with setbacks, victories, and those unexpected moments of clarity that make you pause and smile. As I rebuilt my life, I realized that evolving relationships were as crucial to my healing as any physical recovery.

Every relationship—whether with a friend, my spouse, or a family member—brought its unique challenges and rewards. Some days, the emotional weight felt almost too heavy to bear, and at times, the support I needed seemed just out of reach. But in those moments, I discovered a resilience I never knew I had. I learned that asking for help didn't mean losing my independence and that vulnerability, far from being a weakness, could be a source of strength.

Looking back, I see how much my relationships have changed— not in ways I expected but in ways that have made me appreciate the people who chose to stay, who chose to walk this path with me, even when it wasn't easy.

Because in the end, that's what love—true love, in all its forms—is all about.

CHAPTER 15:
A NEW BEGINNING

Embracing the Ebb and Flow of Healing

As I look back on the journey that has shaped me, it's easy to see the ebb and flow of light and darkness, of hope and despair, of love and loss. It's a reminder that life is never as linear as we'd like it to be. We move through moments of clarity, only to be pulled back into confusion; we embrace healing, yet find ourselves revisiting old wounds. This is the rhythm of life—a constant shifting between highs and lows.

What I've come to realize is that the challenges we face are not simply obstacles to overcome—they are part of our story. They shape us, mold us, and sometimes even break us. But through it all, I have learned that it's not the challenges themselves that define us; it's how we rise from them, how we transform in the face of adversity. Healing is not a final destination. It is an ongoing journey that doesn't follow a straight line but instead bends and twists with every passing day. And sometimes, those twists take us into places we didn't expect.

The Road to Self-Discovery

One of the hardest lessons I've learned through my pain and loss is that healing doesn't happen overnight. It's not something you can rush or force. It's a gradual process, often one step forward and two steps back. But in each of those steps, there is growth. I've learned to be kinder to myself, to allow myself time to grieve, to heal, and to simply *be*.

Loss—whether it's the death of someone close to you, a major life change, or the loss of health—has a way of shaking us to our core. It challenges the very fabric of who we are. But as I've come to understand, loss doesn't have to be the end of our story; it can be the beginning of something new. It may not feel like it at first, but it's in those moments of devastation that we often find the greatest potential for growth.

There were times when I felt lost in the aftermath of everything that had happened to me—when my body betrayed me, when I felt disconnected from the world I once knew, and when I struggled to find purpose. But looking back now, I see how those moments of uncertainty were essential. They forced me to slow down, to reassess, to redefine what it meant to live a meaningful life.

Redefining Strength and Success

What I didn't realize amid my grief and pain was how much strength I had within me. It's easy to forget how resilient we are when we're consumed by sorrow, but we are capable of far

more than we give ourselves credit for. We can bend without breaking, weather the storm, and heal and rebuild, often without even realizing how much strength we have accumulated along the way.

I also had to redefine my understanding of success. Before my accident, success was tied to external achievements—career milestones, personal accolades, and the ability to *do* and *accomplish* without limitation. But now, success looks different.

Success is getting out of bed on the hard days.

Success is allowing myself to rest without guilt.

Success is creating art, even when my hands ache.

Success is showing up for myself, even when I don't feel like it.

This shift in perspective didn't happen overnight. It took years of unlearning old patterns, of challenging the internal voice that told me I wasn't enough unless I was constantly doing. But now, I see success not as a finish line but as something fluid—something that evolves as I do.

The Strength in Vulnerability

I also learned that it's okay to ask for help. There is this common misconception that seeking help is a sign of weakness, that somehow, we should be able to handle everything on our own. But the truth is, we don't have to face our struggles alone. Sometimes, the most empowering thing we can do is reach out to others—to lean on our loved ones, to seek support, and to allow ourselves to be vulnerable.

There is incredible strength in vulnerability. It's not a sign of failure to ask for help; it's a sign of wisdom. Recognizing when we need others and allowing them to be there for us is an act of courage. It's a choice to step into the light rather than retreat into the shadows. For years, I prided myself on my independence. I thought that strength meant handling everything alone. But through my journey, I've come to see that true strength lies in connection—in the willingness to be seen, to be supported, to be held in the moments when we feel like we are falling apart.

Finding Joy in the Unexpected

One of the most surprising parts of this journey has been learning how to find joy in places I never expected. Before my accident, joy was something I took for granted. I assumed it came from big moments— milestones, achievements, external validation. But in the aftermath of loss and change, I've discovered that joy is often found in the smallest, simplest things.

Joy is feeling the sun on my face after a long winter.

Joy is a quiet morning with a cup of coffee and a blank canvas.

Joy is the way my dog, Anna, rests her head on my lap, trusting and content.

Joy is laughter with friends who have walked through the fire with me and stayed.

I used to believe that joy had to be earned—that I had to deserve happiness. But now, I see that joy is always available to us, even in the darkest of times. It doesn't erase pain, but it reminds us that there is still light, still beauty, still life waiting to be lived.

A New Chapter, A New Perspective

Now, as I reflect on who I am today versus who I was before my accident and my diagnosis, I can see just how far I've come. I may not be the same person I was before, but that doesn't mean I've lost anything. I've gained something far more valuable: an understanding of my strength. An understanding that my struggles don't define me; they shape me. They teach me. They allow me to inspire others to find their strength, to move beyond surviving and begin *thriving*.

Healing isn't about going back to who we were before. It's about embracing who we are *now*—with our scars, lessons, resilience, and all. And so, as I step into this new chapter of my life, I do so with a heart that has been broken but mended, with hands that may ache but still create, and with a spirit that has been tested but refuses to break.

I am no longer just enduring life. I am *living* it, in my way, at my own pace. And through it all, I've learned that the most beautiful thing we can do is embrace both our vulnerability and our resilience.

We ***can*** be soft and strong.

We ***can*** be broken and whole.

We ***can*** heal and thrive, not despite our struggles, but *because* of them.

And I hope that in sharing my journey, others will find the courage to face their battles and discover the strength that lies within them, waiting to emerge.

CHAPTER 16: FINDING JOY IN NEW WAYS

Redefining Happiness

One of the hardest parts of my recovery was accepting that some things would never be the same. Certain activities, movements, and expectations had to be adjusted. But rather than focus on what I had lost, I started to explore what I could still do. It wasn't easy at first— change rarely is—but it was necessary.

Joy had always been something I associated with movement, control, and the ability to create without limits. Before the accident, happiness felt effortless. It came in the form of spontaneous adventures, long hours spent painting without pain, and the rush of a fast-paced career. But in the wake of trauma, my relationship with happiness changed. I found myself searching for it in places I had never looked before, and in doing so, I learned that joy is not something we wait for—it's something we actively seek.

Finding Comfort in Small Moments

At first, I mourned the life I had before. I grieved the ease with which I used to move, the ability to create without limitation, and the freedom of an unburdened body. But as time went on, I realized that my life hadn't ended—it had shifted. With that shift came the opportunity to redefine what happiness looked like.

I started noticing the smaller joys:

The warmth of the morning sun streaming through the window as I sipped my coffee.

The comfort of my dogs, curling up beside me, sensing when I needed their presence the most.

The satisfaction of creating art in new ways, even if it meant using unconventional tools.

The laughter shared with friends who understood my warped sense of humor.

The simple beauty of breathing in fresh air after days spent resting.

These moments weren't grand or life-altering on their own, but they added up. They became the foundation upon which I built my new life— a life that, while different, was still worth living.

The Evolution of My Creative Process

Art had always been a source of joy for me. It was my passion, my career, my way of making sense of the world. But after the accident and my diagnosis of CAPS, my hands no longer worked the way they once had. Holding a paintbrush for extended periods became painful, and I had to confront the possibility that my artistic process would never be the same.

For a while, I resisted change. I kept trying to work the way I always had, pushing through the discomfort, refusing to acknowledge that my body had different needs now. But denial only led to frustration, and frustration threatened to steal the joy that art had always given me.

So, I adapted.

I experimented with new tools—palette knives, cake piping bags, and unconventional textures that allowed me to create without relying on fine motor skills. I embraced abstraction, letting my emotions dictate the flow of my work rather than clinging to the precision I had once valued. And in that shift, something incredible happened.

My art became more expressive, more raw, and more deeply connected to my emotions than ever before. It was no longer about recreating the past; it was about embracing the present.

That realization—that my creativity wasn't limited by my physical abilities but only by my willingness to evolve—became one of the most liberating moments of my journey.

Learning to Move Again at My Own Pace

Movement had always been second nature to me, something I

never had to think twice about. But after the accident and the years that followed, even the simplest motions felt foreign. My body no longer responded the way I expected it to, and every step felt uncertain.

At first, I resented my body for what it had lost. I longed to move freely, without pain, without the constant awareness of my limitations. But over time, I began to shift my perspective. Instead of focusing on what I couldn't do, I started celebrating what I *could* do.

A short walk with minimal pain became a victory.

Stretching in the morning without stiffness felt like an accomplishment.

Standing a little longer each day reminded me that progress, no matter how slow, was still progress.

I stopped comparing myself to the person I used to be and started appreciating the person I was becoming. My body had been through hell, and yet, it was still carrying me forward.

That, in itself, was something to be grateful for.

The Role of Gratitude in Finding Joy

For a long time, I thought happiness was something that just *happened* to people. But in the wake of trauma, I learned that joy is something we must actively cultivate. One of the most powerful tools for doing so is gratitude.

At first, gratitude felt forced. How could I be grateful

when my body hurt? When my life had changed so drastically? When so many things had been taken from me? But the more I practiced it, the more I realized that gratitude wasn't about ignoring my pain—it was about acknowledging what was *still* good.

Each night, I started writing down three things I was grateful for. Some days, they were big things—support from loved ones, a breakthrough in my art, a moment of relief from pain. Other days, they were small—a particularly good cup of tea, the sound of rain, a quiet moment of peace.

Over time, this practice rewired my brain. I started *looking* for joy rather than waiting for it to find me. And in doing so, I discovered that even on the hardest days, there was always something to be grateful for.

Rebuilding My Identity

Perhaps the most challenging part of this journey was learning to see myself in a new light. I had spent so many years defining myself by my abilities, my career, my independence. When those things changed, I felt lost. Who was I if I wasn't the same artist, the same physically capable person, the same version of myself I had always known?

It took time—years, even—but I eventually realized that my worth had never been tied to those things. I was not just my career. I was not just my physical abilities. I was *more* than what I could do.

I ***was*** my resilience.

I ***was*** my creativity.

I ***was*** my kindness, my passion, my ability to adapt and grow.

Rebuilding my identity wasn't about returning to who I had been— it was about embracing who I was becoming. And in that acceptance, I found peace.

Embracing the Unknown

If there's one thing I've learned, it's that life rarely goes as planned. It twists, it turns, and it throws challenges our way that we never saw coming. But in those challenges, there is opportunity—the opportunity to grow, to evolve, to find joy in ways we never expected. I wouldn't have chosen this path. I wouldn't have asked for the accident, for the diagnosis, for the hardships that followed. But standing where I am now, I can say with certainty that I *have* chosen how to respond.

I ***have*** chosen to adapt.

I ***have*** chosen to seek joy.

I ***have*** chosen to keep moving forward, even when the way is uncertain.

And that, I've learned, is what truly matters.

This is my life now. And I am learning to embrace it.

CHAPTER 17:

EMBRACING CHANGE – THE ART OF LETTING GO

The Fear of Change

Change is one of those things that we're constantly told is inevitable, but knowing that doesn't make it any easier to accept. There's something deeply unsettling about realizing that life as you knew it no longer exists in the same way. It happens in big, dramatic moments—an accident, a diagnosis, the loss of someone you love— but it also happens quietly, in the small shifts that you don't even notice at first.

After my accident, change wasn't something I had the option of resisting. It was forced upon me. My body was different. My mind was different. My relationships were different. Nothing felt familiar anymore. And for a long time, that terrified me.

I wanted to cling to the past, to hold onto the person I had been before. I kept trying to do things the way I used to, refusing to acknowledge that my body had limits now, that my emotions were more fragile, that my worldview had been altered. I thought if I fought hard enough, I could make everything go back to the way it was before. But that's not how life works. The more I resisted change, the harder it became to move forward.

I was stuck, constantly looking backward, constantly measuring my current self against a version of me that no longer existed. And it wasn't until I started to let go—really let go—that I realized change wasn't something to fear. It was something to embrace.

The Art of Letting Go

Letting go is not a single moment. It's not as simple as deciding,

Okay, I'm done with the past. Time to move on. If only it were that easy.

Letting go is a process, a daily choice. Some days, it feels liberating. Other days, it feels like grief. There were moments when I felt relief in accepting my new reality, in finding new ways to create, to live, to love. Then there were days when I would be blindsided by sadness, longing for the life I used to have, mourning the loss of what could have been. I had to teach myself how to let go in layers.

Letting Go of Expectations – I had always been someone who made plans, who envisioned my future in crisp detail. When life took a sharp detour, those plans shattered. I had to learn to let go of the expectation that my life would unfold in a specific way.

Letting Go of Guilt – Survivor's guilt, grief, and self-blame became frequent visitors in my mind. I had to remind myself—over and over—that letting go of the past didn't mean forgetting it. It didn't mean I was dismissing my pain. It simply meant that I wasn't allowing it to control me anymore.

Letting Go of the Need for Control – This was the hardest. Before, I found comfort in structure, in knowing what was coming next. But life had proven to me that control was an illusion. In learning to release my grip, I discovered something unexpected- freedom.

Letting go doesn't mean erasing the past. It means making peace with it.

Finding Growth in Uncertainty

The most profound lesson I learned in this journey was that growth and comfort rarely coexist. Real transformation happens in discomfort, in uncertainty, in the moments where you feel like you have no idea what comes next.

At first, this terrified me. The unknown had always felt dangerous, like stepping into a dark room without knowing what was inside. But over time, I started to shift my perspective.

What if the unknown wasn't something to fear?

What if, instead, it was filled with possibilities I hadn't yet considered?

The truth is, had my life gone exactly as I planned, I

wouldn't be the person I am today. I wouldn't have discovered new ways to create, new depths of resilience, and new connections with people who truly saw me. I wouldn't have learned how to adapt, how to build a life that honored both my past and my future.

Change isn't just something that happens to us. It's something we can grow through.

Rebuilding Myself, Piece by Piece

One of the hardest parts of embracing change was realizing that I had to rebuild myself from the ground up. The person I had been before didn't exist anymore, and while that was painful to accept, it also gave me a unique opportunity—to redefine who I wanted to be. Instead of focusing on what I had lost, I started asking myself:

Who am I now?

What do I still love?

How can I take what I've been through and turn it into something meaningful?

Slowly, I started to answer those questions.

I found new ways to create, experimenting with textures and techniques that accommodated my body's limitations. I started writing more, using words to process the emotions I struggled to say out loud. I leaned into my relationships, prioritizing the people who had stayed and who had supported me when I felt unlovable.

I wasn't the same. But I was still *me*.

Embracing the Beauty of Change

If you had told me years ago that I would one day find peace in the changes that once broke me, I wouldn't have believed you. But now, I see things differently. Change is painful, yes. But it is also beautiful.

It is the moment a caterpillar becomes a butterfly, not without struggle, but with the promise of something new.

It is the shifting of the seasons, the slow transformation of winter into spring.

It is the breaking of something old so that something new can take its place.

For so long, I thought my story was about loss. About what had been taken from me, about the ways my life had been altered without my consent. But now, I see that my story isn't just about loss.

It's about *becoming*.

It's about learning to embrace the unknown, to trust that even in the hardest moments, something is waiting on the other side. It's about finding strength in the spaces where we once felt broken.

Change is not the enemy. It is the gateway to something new. And as I step into this next chapter of my life, I do so with open hands, ready to embrace whatever comes next.

Final Thoughts: Moving Forward Without Fear

If you are reading this and struggling with change, if you feel stuck between who you were and who you are becoming, know this:

You are ***not*** alone.

You are allowed to grieve the past while still embracing the future. You are capable of more than you realize.

Change is scary. But it is also a gift.

So, take a deep breath. Let go of what no longer serves you. And trust that something beautiful is waiting just ahead.

You are still writing your story. And it is far from over.

CHAPTER 18:
ART AS A SYMBOL OF RECOVERY

The accident stole five years from my hands. Five years of trying— desperately—to make a mark on paper, only to watch my efforts crumble under the weight of my body's betrayal. My hand no longer felt like my own. The fluidity I once had with a brush, the ease of a pencil gliding across paper, was replaced with stiffness, pain, and an unrelenting disconnect between mind and muscle. It was as if my brain spoke one language and my hands another, neither understanding the other's intent. I tried everything. I sat at my desk, sketchbook open, willing my fingers to remember. But every line came out jagged, and every attempt to capture what lived in my mind fell short, distorted and unrecognizable. Frustration built. It wasn't just about making art—it was about losing a part of myself. The part that had been there since childhood, the part that gave me solace, identity, and purpose.

By the end of 2018, I was at my lowest. The weight of everything— the accident, the endless doctor visits, the financial strain of medical bills—pressed down on me. I had spent so long trying to force my art back into the shape it once held, like trying to fit into an old coat that no longer matched the body it belonged to. And then, in that moment of exhaustion, I stopped trying to make what was familiar. I gave in to what was raw, what was real.

That's when *11:04* was born.

It was different from anything I had ever painted before. The delicate watercolor strokes I had mastered in college were nowhere to be found. Instead, I layered pieces of my reality—fragments of doctor's notes, the accident report, medical bills—all woven into the fabric of the canvas. These were the remnants of my suffering, now repurposed as something tangible, something I could control. I slathered paint over them, not with a careful brush, but with whatever tools I could grasp—palette knives, my fingers, anything that allowed me to translate what words could not. It was chaotic, unfiltered, and for the first time in years, it felt true.

At that moment, something shifted. My hands still fought me, but I found new ways to move forward. The precision I once had was gone, but in its place was something more visceral, more instinctual. I experimented—cake piping bags replaced fine brushes, allowing me to create fluidity without requiring a steady grip. Palette knives scraped and spread paint in ways I had never considered before. I let go of perfection and embraced expression. That night, as I stepped back to look at *11:04*, I realized I had done something I hadn't been able to do in five years. I had created. And in that creation, I reclaimed a piece of myself.

This was no longer just about adapting—it was about transformation. My art was no longer confined to the techniques I had once known. It became something new, just as I had.

I was not the same artist I was before the accident.

I was something else entirely. And that was okay.

CHAPTER 19:
A SMALL MOMENT - A BIG WIN

The morning light filters through the window, casting a golden glow across my studio. The familiar ache in my hands lingers, a reminder of the battles I have fought, but I no longer resent it. It is simply part of me now, woven into the fabric of my existence, as much a part of my story as the art I create.

I take a deep breath and press forward, picking up the palette knife with steady fingers. The colors come to life under my touch, textured strokes layering atop one another, each carrying the weight of a past I have come to accept. For years, I believed healing meant returning to who I once was. That if I pushed hard enough, fought long enough, I could reclaim the life I lost. But I have learned that healing is not about reclaiming—it is about becoming.

The door creaks open behind me. Ken leans against the frame, his eyes warm, understanding. He doesn't have to ask if I'm okay; he already knows.

"How's it going?" he asks softly.

I glance at the painting before me, then back at him. "Different." He steps closer, studying the piece. "Good different?"

I nod, exhaling slowly. "Yeah. I think so."

The silence between us is comfortable, filled with an unspoken knowing. He has walked this road with me, held my hand through the worst of it, and never once let go. I think of the others who have been there, too—my family, my friends, the strangers who became lifelines in my darkest moments. And I think of those I have lost, whose absence lingers like a whisper in the wind.

I set the knife down and step back, tilting my head as I take in the canvas before me. It is imperfect and raw but full of life. Full of survival. It is a reflection of me, of the person I have become—not despite the pain, but because of it.

Closing my eyes, I hear his voice, clear and steady, just as it was on that day when everything seemed to slow.

This, too, shall pass.

The words settle into my bones, not as a fleeting reassurance, but as a truth that has carried me through every moment of fear, every setback, every uncertainty. The pain passed. The fear passed. The grief passed. And even when they return, they do not stay. They never stay. I open my eyes and reach for the palette knife again, my hands no longer trembling. There is still more to create, more to say, more life to live. Because this, too, shall pass.

And what comes next is mine to define.

EPILOGUE:
THIS TOO SHALL PASS

There are moments in life that redefine us. Moments that fracture time into *before* and *after*, leaving us to pick up the pieces of who we once were, trying to make sense of what remains. My accident was one of those moments. My diagnosis was another. Loss has carved its way through my life more times than I can count. Each time, it left me staring at an unfamiliar version of myself in the mirror, wondering if I would ever recognize the person looking back.

And yet, through it all, one lesson has remained— *this too shall pass.*

These words, spoken by my grandfather in the moments when I needed them most, have been my anchor and my guiding light. They have been both a comfort and a challenge. A reminder that pain is not permanent, that even the darkest nights eventually give way to morning. But they are also a call to action—a promise that if I keep moving forward, if I refuse to let hardship define me, I will emerge stronger on the other side.

For a long time, I resisted the idea of healing. Not because I didn't want to heal, but because I thought healing meant erasing the past, undoing the damage, returning to the version of myself that existed before everything fell apart. I fought to reclaim what had been taken from me, refusing to accept that some things—some versions of ourselves—are meant to be left behind. But healing is not about going back. It is about becoming. It is about taking every scar, every loss, every lesson, and using them to build something new.

I have come to understand that healing is not a destination but a journey, an unfolding path that is never truly finished. Some days, the weight of the past feels unbearable. Some days, I wake up, and the pain— the physical, the emotional, the echoes of everything I have endured— makes it hard to move forward. But I have also learned that strength is not the absence of struggle. Strength is the decision to keep going, even when it would be easier to give up.

There was a time when I believed that survival meant enduring alone and that asking for help was a sign of weakness. But the truth is, survival is a collective effort. We do not heal in isolation. We heal in connection with those who show up for us in the moments when we cannot stand on our own. We heal in the quiet understanding of a loved one's presence, in the laughter shared in sorrow, in the small victories that remind us that we are still here, still moving forward, still *becoming*.

My grandfather's words were never meant to dismiss pain or to rush the process of healing. He wasn't telling me that suffering was insignificant or that I should simply wait for it to disappear. He was reminding me that no feeling—no matter how intense, no matter how unbearable—lasts forever. Even when life feels insurmountable, change is inevitable. That even the heaviest burdens will shift over time.

I used to think that to honor my survival, I had to justify it. I thought I had to prove that my life was worth saving, that I had to accomplish something extraordinary to make my second chance count. But I see now that the greatest way to honor life is to *live it*—not perfectly, not without struggle, but fully. To wake up each day and choose to move forward, even if it's just one step at a time. To find joy in the small moments. To love deeply. To embrace the uncertainty of it all.

I have spent years carrying the weight of survivor's guilt, questioning why I was given more time when so many others were not. But I have come to understand that the question is not *why was I spared?* But rather *what will I do with the time I have been given?* And I have made my choice.

I will keep going. I will keep growing. And I will keep living.

Because this life—messy, unpredictable, heartbreaking as it is—is still worth living. There is beauty to be found even in the ruins. There is strength in the broken places. There is love that endures beyond loss. And even in the moments when everything feels impossible, when the weight of the past feels too heavy to bear, I will remember my grandfather's words.

This, too, shall pass.

ACKNOWLEDGEMENTS

No journey—especially one of healing and self-discovery—is ever taken alone. While this memoir is deeply personal, I would not have been able to write it, let alone live it, without the unwavering support, expertise, and compassion of the medical professionals who walked alongside me.

To Dr. Adarsh Gupta, Neuropsychology, who unknowingly planted the seed for this memoir—your encouragement and insight gave me the confidence to put my story into words. Thank you for seeing the value in my journey before I could fully recognize it myself. To Dr. Mark Tan, Rheumatologist, who took the time to piece together the complex puzzle that led to my CAPS diagnosis—your patience, dedication, and brilliance changed my life. To you and your staff, thank you for always bringing a smile to my face, even when I was sitting in a chair for four-hour infusions.

To Dr. Mark Gudesblatt, Neurologist, for helping me understand dysautonomia, Sjögren's syndrome, and neuropathy—

"Oh, what a relief it is" to finally have answers. Your guidance helped me navigate a path I never expected to walk, and for that, I am forever grateful.

To Dr. Alan Ettinger, Neurologist, who taught me that knowledge is power when it comes to managing my seizures. Your expertise gave me the tools to take control of my health in ways I never imagined possible.

To Dr. Eva Greco, Therapist, for reminding me that it was okay to feel everything I was experiencing. You provided me with the tools to navigate some of the darkest days of my life, and because of you, I found my way forward.

To Dr. Bradley Meltzer, Neuro-Optometrist, for being there from the earliest days of my visual therapy—thank you for creating a safe space, for the laughs and chats about just about anything, and for always suggesting what's best to help me see properly. I know that whatever you recommend will always be worth it!

To Dr. Richard Block & Dr. Derek Silverman, the men who quite literally got me back on my feet—thank you for helping me not just to stand again, but to walk down the aisle. Your care and dedication gave me a moment I will cherish forever.

To Dr. Michael Wirth and the staff at Pinnacle Physical Therapy, for guiding me through the ups and downs of recovery. Your encouragement, patience, and expertise helped me regain the strength I thought I had lost.

Each of you has played a profound role in my journey, and there are no words that can fully express my gratitude. Thank you for believing in me, for fighting alongside me, and for reminding me, in your own ways, that healing is possible.

ABOUT THE AUTHOR

Loretta A. Oberheim is an artist, writer, and survivor who has turned her journey of resilience into a source of inspiration for others. After surviving a near-fatal car accident, she faced years of recovery, battling PTSD, chronic illness, and the emotional weight of survivor's guilt. Diagnosed with Cryopyrin- Associated Periodic Syndrome (CAPS), a rare autoinflammatory disease, she continues to navigate life with strength and purpose. Through her writing and advocacy, Loretta shares her story to encourage others facing trauma, grief, and chronic illness. She believes in the power of storytelling, art, and community as tools for healing. When she's not writing, she can be found creating in her art studio, spending time with her husband, Kenny, and her beloved rescue dogs.

THIS TOO SHALL PASS:
A Memoir of Survival, Loss, and Finding Purpose

Hey, you found me!

Since you're here, I just want to take a moment to remind you of something important—**you're doing great.** Seriously.

Life has its ups and downs, and I know some moments feel heavier than others. But whatever you're going through, **it's temporary.** Just like the good times don't last forever, neither do the tough ones.

So take a deep breath. Give yourself a high-five (yes, really—go for it). And remember: **You've got this.**

Keep going. Keep shining. The world is better with you in it.

<3

www.ingramcontent.com/pod-product-compliance
Lightning Source LLC
LaVergne TN
LVHW041708060526
838201LV00043B/629